To Carolyn & Phil
Merry Christmas 2009

Phil, Jeanne & Yoki

Love Heels

Love
Heels

Tales from
Canine Companions
for Independence

By Patricia Dibsie | Foreword by Dean Koontz

YORKVILLE PRESS
NEW YORK, NEW YORK

Library of Congress Cataloging-in-Publication Data

Dibsie, Patricia.
Love heels : tales from Canine Companions for Independence / Patricia Dibsie.
p. cm.
ISBN 0-9729427-2-6
1. Dogs--United States--Anecdotes. 2. Dog owners--United
States--Anecdotes. 3. Dogs--Social aspects--United States--Anecdotes.
4. Dogs--Therapeutic use--United States--Anecdotes. 5. Canine
Companions for Independence (Firm) I. Canine Companions for
Independence (Firm) II. Title.
SF426.2.D52 2003
636.7'088--dc21
2003006935

Designed by Tina Taylor
Printed in China by Asia Pacific Offset

jes 10 9 8 7 6 5 4 3 2 1

CANINE COMPANIONS
FOR INDEPENDENCE

Dedication

This book is dedicated to CCI graduates.
Your courage, determination, spirit, and
the powerful bond you share with your Canine
Companions is our daily inspiration.

Contents

Foreword

Dean Koontz

Once, when my wife, Gerda, and I were visiting the Canine Companions for Independence facility in Oceanside, California, the director—at that time a wonderful, dedicated woman named Judi Pierson—encouraged me to enter the exercise yard associated with the kennels, whereupon perhaps two dozen golden retriever puppies exploded out of concealment and raced toward me with ear-flopping excitement. I dropped to my knees, and this furry swarm of three-month-old cuties climbed all over me, until I appeared to be wearing a coat with twenty-four twitching tails. Bliss.

The special, wonderful, and deeply mysterious relationship between dogs and human beings has been chronicled since the beginning of recorded history. In bleak and inhospitable ancient times, in their caves and crude huts, men and women shared with dogs the night watch for predators, and took heart from one another when the odds against survival seemed insurmountable. For thousands of years, dogs have worked with us as shepherds, as sentinels, as trackers . . . and they have raced joyfully with us across open fields, splashed happily with us in rivers, lakes. More than one animal behaviorist has written that dogs and human beings are the only two species that remain interested in games and play for their entire life spans: In other words, both dogs and human beings keep in their hearts the memory and innocence of childhood for as long as they live.

In 1870, Senator George Vest wrote, in part: "The only absolutely unselfish friend that man can have in this selfish world, the one that never proves ungrateful or treacherous, is his dog. A man's dog stands by him in prosperity and in poverty, in health and in sickness. He will sleep on the cold ground, where the wintry winds blow and the snow drives fiercely, if only he may be near his master's side." Although some people respond to a dog's unconditional love with indifference or even cruelty, each time someone repays a dog's devotion with respect and affection, there ensues a relationship both ennobling and magical.

Our friends and neighbors with disabilities who come to CCI with the hope of improving their lives are among the most courageous people I have ever known. Although life has presented them with problems that might break many, these seekers are not broken. They are determinedly optimistic in the face of adversity, hopeful when others might have lost all hope, and frequently more attuned to the beauty and the joy of life than are those fortunate enough to have the use of all their limbs. In my book, their indomitability makes each of them a hero.

When they arrive at CCI, they expect to change their lives for the better. They know that the challenge of learning to handle and to live with an assistance dog will be met only with hard work and perseverance, and they are usually a little scared. Until they are overcome by the experience, however, they often don't realize that the relationships they are about to embark upon with their four-legged companions will not merely make the tasks of daily life easier to accomplish but will be inspiring, even spiritual, and filled with wonder. Providing life-changing service to a disabled man or woman, each dog seems to *know* that it is fulfilling a role that has been the destiny of its kind since the morning of creation, and it takes obvious satisfaction and pleasure in its good work. The bond between each CCI graduate and his or her special dog is one that, to a perceptive observer, reveals profound meaning and mysterious depths in our existence.

In my faith, there is a tradition that says we cannot redeem the world by pursuing grand utopian schemes; rather all of us must brighten the corner where we live, and by uncountable acts of kindness, small and large, press back the darkness. Canine Companions for Independence—its founders, its employees, the thousands who donate time or money, or both, to the organization nationwide, the persons with disabilities and their families who come here with the intention of improving their lives—brightens every corner where it operates and daily redeems our troubled world. May God bless everyone associated with CCI; as for the dogs—they don't need blessing, for they are pure of heart and guaranteed the reward of Heaven's fields from the day that each is born.

Dean Koontz

Dean Koontz

Jean Schulz

I became involved with CCI because I was fascinated by both the simplicity and the complexity of providing highly trained service dogs to those who need them. I soon came to realize the richness of the many people I met through CCI—everyone was immersed in his own joyful work, focused on a single goal.

The magic of CCI really came home to me, though, when I received a letter from a professor I had much admired when I was in college. It was thirty years later, and he told me of his young granddaughter who was matched with a CCI dog. He and his wife wanted to tell me how it had changed their family. Not too long after that, I learned that the adult daughter of one of my husband's friends from his Saint Paul days had a CCI dog that truly was a lifesaver for her. This was more than a coincidence. It showed me how broad the net of CCI stretches and how our lives intersect. When people ask me about my involvement with CCI, I can honestly say that it makes my life better every day. The reality of CCI centers around the love that develops between dogs and people. It is an antidote to the negativity in the world.

In this book, Patricia Dibsie paints a beautiful picture full of small incidents that truly color life. Some of these stories will make you laugh, and some of them may make you cry. But they will all make your day.

Jean Schulz, President
Canine Companions for Independence

Jean Schulz

A Message from the Executive Director

Corey Hudson

Canine Companions for Independence (CCI), founded in 1975 in Santa Rosa, California, is a family of dedicated people who thrive on helping others by raising and training wonderful and talented dogs to assist people with disabilities. Building on the model of the guide dog, its earliest workers, who were all volunteers, not only trained the dogs but also placed, or teamed, them with those who needed their help. From its modest beginnings CCI has grown to include five regional centers, augmented by thirty volunteer chapters, to serve the whole country. The regional center, which oversees all those in its area who are involved in the creation of a Canine Companion, is where the dogs are teamed with their human charges and where the teams are trained.

Today CCI is a 501(c)(3) nonprofit organization that is funded by private contributions and receives no government support. The organization employs a paid staff for administrative, training, and veterinary services; the majority of its workers, however, are volunteers. CCI graduates do not pay for their service dogs. They are asked to pay

"Some people wait a lifetime for a miracle . . .
We raise them one at a time." —Canine Companions for Independence

only a $100 team-training registration fee, which is reimbursed in supplies. Once a team has graduated from the training program, instructors and other program staff provide ongoing support to ensure quality partnerships. CCI is proud that it was the first assistance dog organization to be accredited by Assistance Dog International, and it leads the way in promoting cooperative efforts between many of the new and developing assistance dog organizations.

Under the leadership of National President Jean Schulz, CCI took a huge step forward in the late 1980s. Its success can be gauged by the fact that since that time CCI has doubled the number of assistance dog teams placed each year and now conducts more than 500 follow-up visits a year. In addition, CCI has seen a huge growth in its assets.

In the past twelve years the organization has enlarged the team concept to include hearing teams and facility teams, along with a special category called skilled companion team. The latter category was created to serve children and others needing the assistance of a third party. This period has also seen the enlistment of CCI graduates to serve

on all five regional advisory boards as well as on the CCI National Board of Directors, helping to promote self-advocacy and a partnership of trust and caring between the agency and those it serves.

The Jean and Charles Schulz Campus, located in Santa Rosa, serves as CCI's national headquarters as well as its Northwest Regional Center. In addition, CCI has opened the Dean and Gerda Koontz Campus (Southwest Regional Center) in Oceanside, California; the Anheuser-Busch/SeaWorld Campus (Southeast Regional Center) in Orlando, Florida; the Northeast Regional Center in Farmingdale, New York; and the North Central Regional Center in Delaware, Ohio. CCI is currently assessing the need for a sixth center, to be located in the Rocky Mountain region. There are two satellite offices, one located in Colorado Springs, Colorado, and the other in Chicago, Illinois.

In my capacity as executive director, I have seen over and over again how the interdependence between dog and human created at CCI enriches the lives of both. To be part of an organization that provides such a vital service is a great privilege for me, as it is for all of us at CCI who raise miracles one at a time.

Corey Hudson, Executive Director
Canine Companions for Independence

LOVE HEELS • Tales from Canine Companions for Independence

Breeder Caretakers

Once you've been a part of the miracle, it's something you want to share.

Breeder Caretakers Only those dogs that meet Canine Companions for Independence's high standards for temperament and physical health and strength are chosen to become breeders of future Canine Companions. These dogs, both male and female, are placed with individuals or families known as breeder caretakers, who oversee the pregnancy of the female dogs and the whelping and raising of the puppies. Once a female dog has whelped up to five litters, she is spayed and remains with the breeder caretaker as a pet.

It's a Boy, Boy, Boy, Girl...

Many people asked Cathy Phillips for a sneak peek into the everyday moments before, during, and after the birth of a litter. And so she obliged; she penned her thoughts and feelings daily in e-mails and sent them out to interested CCI puppy raisers and supporters. The journals have been a huge hit, not only with those who received the initial postings but also with friends and families who got the missives secondhand. Her fan club has grown, doubled, tripled, and spiraled out of control.

"It is good to have an end to journey toward; but it is the journey that matters, in the end." —Ursula K. Le Guin

Cathy grins but understands. Once you've been a part of the miracle, it's something you want to share. What follows below is an edited version of the dozens of pages from Cathy's journals about her breeder Corette, which she began writing in the spring of 2001.

Thursday, May 3: Cory was bred three times over the weekend to Lakota. I will drive up to Santa Rosa to pick her up next week. I miss that silly little dog! So, counting sixty-three days from when she was bred, that puts her having puppies just about the first of July. We will have her checked at the end of the month by "palpation," a procedure in which the vet ever so gently squeezes her tummy to feel for signs of fetuses. She also will have an ultrasound, and that is SO cool. If she is pregnant, we will be able to see a puppy heartbeat on the ultrasound! I get goose bumps whenever I hear the sound of a teeny-tiny puppy heart beating inside its mama!

Tuesday, May 15: Very interesting! Cory did NOT want to eat breakfast at all this morning! Wonder if this is the start of morning sickness? Also interesting, Cory was totally glued to me and stayed that way all night.

Thursday, May 17: Cory is definitely much more subdued than her usual happy, silly, outgoing self. I do think that Cory IS pregnant and we will know one way or another in four DAYS!!!!!! C'mon, Cory! Puppies, puppies, puppies, puppies, puppies, puppies, puppies, puppies, puppies, puppies! Happy, healthy, working puppies!!!!!!!!!!!

Friday, May 25:
Yahooooooooooooooooooooo!!!! Little Miss Cory is pregnant! I knew it! This is so exciting! CORY-BELLE is pregnant!!!!!!!! The vet palpated and did an ultrasound; both confirmed her pregnancy. Since it is still very early in her pregnancy, we were able to see the heartbeats of the puppies but not hear them yet! It is so exciting to see the little itty-bitty hearts beating away! We are guessing that there are six to ten puppies.

Wednesday, May 30: Little Miss Cory is finally getting over her morning sickness. Late last week it actually became "all-day sickness"! She was just not very happy eating anything. She would eat a little bit of chicken, maybe a little liver or cooked ground meat, but she FLATLY refused to eat kibble (though dog cookies were okay!). Am I being manipulated a little??? Maybe, but with six to ten important little lives growing inside her belly, Cory's well-being is of the utmost importance! So I cooked and cajoled.

Sunday, June 3: Cory is doing great. Her tummy is definitely getting rounder. She is finally done with morning sickness, and I am such a happy breeder caretaker today! She is now thirty-five days from her first breeding. Approximately twenty-eight days to go!

In about two weeks, we will set up the "puppy nursery" and start getting Cory used to the idea of being in the whelping pool. She is very snuggly still and is constantly attached to Jim or me. She loves to roll over on her back and get lots of big tummy rubs, always with an ear-to-ear grin on her face!

Wednesday, June 20: It's day 53 of Cory's pregnancy! Wow! It's getting close! We are about ten days from whelping now! YIKES! The whelping room is almost ready. All the little "collars" are cut and ready, scissors for cutting umbilical cords have been cleaned, hemostats are ready to clamp off the cords, the white board is all set up for recording all the necessary information, sheets and towels have been laundered, and the heat lamp and heating pads are ready (if needed). Baby bottles, nipples, goat's milk, supplement—it's all ready if needed. The whelping pool has been cleaned and sanitized and will be set up today.

Friday, June 22: Today we took Cory to the vet to be x-rayed to see how many puppies she REALLY is carrying! Dr. Whalen (whom I love, trust, and respect with all my heart!) brought the x-rays into the room, while his staff loved on Cory. We had seen five or six puppies on the ultrasound but knew there could be more. With a huge smile on his face, he put the x-ray up on the light box and switched it on. Every one of us let out an "OHHHHH" when there were at least eight puppies instantly visible on the x-ray!

I am going to try to keep everyone updated as often as possible. Though this is such an exciting time, I think it is also always a bit of a scary time, too. I want Cory and all the puppies to be okay; I want them here happy and healthy and thriving. So everyone take an extra second to think good thoughts for Cory and her pups.

The puppies began arriving early in the morning on Wednesday, June 27. The next day, a bleary-eyed Cathy sat down at her computer to recap the event.

Thursday, June 28: Hi! Well, I think I am somewhat rested and somewhat coherent. What an incredible experience Cory's whelping was! This is the eighth CCI litter I have whelped and I have never seen a whelping this easy!

Cory was enchanted with her first pup. She kept looking at him and nudging him and cleaning him. Her whole focus was on her boy! I was a little worried that his birth had hurt and scared her a little; my concern was that she be okay with the next pup.

It wasn't long at all before she again got a faraway look in her eyes (it is as if she were totally aware of us, but needed to go to a different place). She began letting out little grunts and moans again. With very little effort, out came puppy number two. No problem, no show of pain or surprise, just stoic Cory doing what she needed to do!

Again, we got the sac off him, cut and tied the umbilical cord and put him with Cory, who now accepted this as totally the norm! After just a few minutes, we

put the first pup back to nurse also. Jim took Cory out for a quick walk while I got the puppy pool cleaned and new newspapers and sheets down.

When Cory is about to have another pup, the preceding puppies go into a "warming box," which is nothing more than a plastic tub with a towel, a heating pad, another towel on the bottom, and then a towel across the top to keep them nice and toasty! Within minutes, puppy number three showed up. Quickly and quietly, he entered the world as a breech birth, but no problems. Cory is getting vanilla ice cream, honey, and Pedialyte to keep her electrolytes up and her blood-sugar level up. She needs this to keep strong during the labor. With just a mild little grunt, puppy number four showed up. Wow, she is really getting into this! Finally a female! I am loving this! At this rate, we were guessing we'd be done by noon. Cory was doing great, resting a little between each pup, drinking water, eating good stuff, and loving on her babies!

Another quick toilet trip for Cory; back into the pool and out came puppy number five. Yikes, she's practically spitting these kids out!

Finally, a bit of a break for Cory, and for us. She got some much needed rest, loved on all the puppies, cleaned them up, and grinned at them like the proudest mom in the world!

We got to get another cup of coffee, get a good look at all the pups, love on them a little ourselves, and tell Cory over and over and over what a wonderful, incredible good girl she was being. She just grinned at us!

In what seemed like no time at all, Cory gave a little grunt. We grabbed the puppies to put them in their warming box and got ready for another pup. Another incredibly easy birth, and out came number six. Cory was now looking like, "What is the big deal here?" She was popping puppies out with great ease. I am so proud of this little girl! WOW! A little bit of nursing time for the sixth pup and some loving from Cory, and then she started grunting again. Good grief! Here comes another! Puppy number seven was a healthy female.

Good grief! Poor Cory. She is so fast at this. She is loving the ice cream and honey and is eagerly lapping up the Pedialyte. What a girl!

It seems like maybe she is done???? We thought we saw eight or nine puppies on the x-ray, but there can be a lot of "shadowing" on the x-rays. We are keeping a very close eye on her, but no contractions happening right away. We clean up the whelping pool, finally get a chance to feed the other dogs, and settle in to see what happens next. Contractions ARE starting again! I have to wonder if this is just a "cleaning out" contraction or if there is an eighth pup in there! I felt a puppy in the birth canal.

This time she was straining harder than we had seen her strain before and she was pretty uncomfortable. This one was taking a while but she was doing great. But I was a little concerned that this might be a REALLY big pup and she would have a hard time delivering him. Not to worry with Miss Cory-Belle! She finally gave a HUGE push and out came number eight. Wow! Not only was he a breech birth, but he was an UPSIDE DOWN breech birth. WHEW! The adrenaline level that you run at during all of this is amazing!

By noon, we were pretty sure she was done. She experienced a couple of very tiny contractions but nothing much. She was so tired; the puppies were nursing happily. She began to doze off and we were more than a little tired ourselves. Quite a day! Glad it is over and the pups are here safe and sound and that Cory is okay. We did a huge cleanup of the whelping room, sat and watched the puppies, and grinned at each other.

Then suddenly, Cory began having a big contraction! Her tail came up as if she were about to deliver another puppy! REALLY, CORY!!!! There was another strong contraction and then, very casually, out slid puppy number nine, another female! I was starting to wonder just HOW many more there might be in there?

No more contractions, no more straining, no more puppies. Cory was done at nine puppies. What a wonderful mom she is already, always loving her puppies. What a girl!

Good night and puppy kisses to all,
Cathy

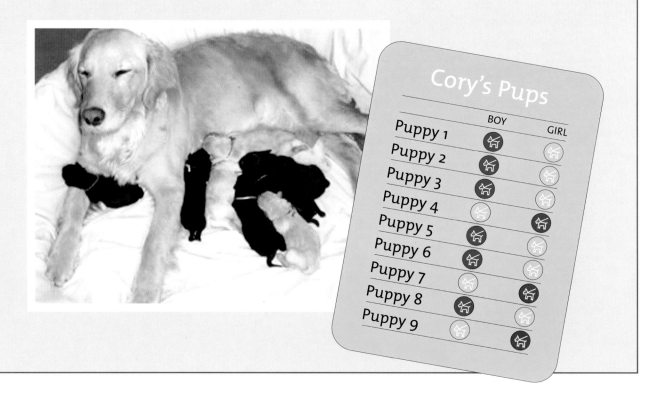

Cory's Pups

	BOY	GIRL
Puppy 1	🐕	
Puppy 2	🐕	
Puppy 3	🐕	
Puppy 4		🐕
Puppy 5	🐕	
Puppy 6	🐕	
Puppy 7		🐕
Puppy 8	🐕	
Puppy 9		🐕

Her Spirit Soars

Cathy Phillips chose to live only because dying would have betrayed the people she had loved and lost. She willed her body to breathe; her spirit to soar.

She wiped the tears from her face and cursed the drunk driver who had stolen everything from her, vowing to live a life large enough to fill four lifetimes. She armed herself with the gentleness of her mother, Aggie Mihalic; the confidence of her husband, Brian Jacklin; and the sheer determination of her best friend, Nancy Landphere. And, only thirty-two years old, she wanted her own life back, too.

Not to forget Kate and Kelly. She never has, to this day. The two Canine Companions for Independence service dog trainees, tethered in the back of the van, were also killed in the horrific wreck en route to the fall 1987 CCI graduation ceremony.

Parts of that fatal afternoon are crystal clear, but a lot has been blurred by pain and horror. Cathy remembers her husband reaching out for her hand, telling her that he was dying. She remembers knowing that Nancy lay dead at the scene. Kate and Kelly died on impact, too. Brian died two hours later at the hospital; her mom died the next morning. Cathy suffered a dislocated right hip and a broken cheekbone. She was released from the hospital two days later.

"The human spirit is stronger than anything that can happen to it." —George C. Scott

The next few years were ugly, she admits. She felt she had nothing to live for and welcomed death. Her survivor's guilt was fueled by anger and resentment as the trial of the drunk driver unfolded. The man had raced away from the scene but was caught later. He was sentenced to three and a half years in prison. That translated into one year and two months for every human life he took. It was something Cathy thought she couldn't live with.

She took her fight to the state government and lobbied for new guidelines that would allow for consecutive, not concurrent, sentencing. She won. She joined MADD and spoke to high school students about the consequences of drinking and driving. Then one day she just got tired of being mad all the time and wanted to leave the anger behind.

Her friends and the animals at her ranch helped Cathy get through the empty days and nights that followed. Staff and volunteers at CCI reached out and pulled her back into their circle. She brought home a third puppy to raise and train.

Slowly, Cathy began to heal. The unconditional love her new puppy showered on her played a big part. That and time. She began to volunteer at the CCI center during team training, helping in any way she could. During lunch and coffee breaks, Cathy talked about the fatal accident and her feelings about what happened. Then she encouraged others to talk about what was going on in their lives. In time, she swapped her deep resentments for an even deeper sense of gratitude. "Some of these people had been through so much more than I could comprehend. Their lives had been physically and emotionally turned inside out and yet they could smile. What they taught me is that a person can get through anything and come out better than ever."

Cathy learned not only to survive but to thrive. Her past is a present she shares to ensure a healthy future. It is a gift, she says, that you can keep only by sharing it with others. So she does, often and unselfishly.

She continued her passion for skydiving and has successfully pulled the cord more than 1,000 times. She met her current husband, Jim Phillips, skydiving. The two decided to tie the knot floating down to earth in a simple ceremony six years ago. And she continues to bring new puppies into her home; she is now raising her twenty-second. As further proof of her dedication, Cathy is one of only three breeder-caretaker teams living more than ninety miles from CCI's national headquarters in Santa Rosa, California. It's an exception, but anyone at CCI can tell you that Cathy Phillips is truly exceptional.

Cathy has had three breeders: Nadia (deceased), Joley (retired), and Cory. In the spring of 2002, Cory had her second litter, and Joley was retired after having had her fifth. In all, Cathy's three bitches have produced eighty-four puppies in ten litters. And that makes her a very proud grandmother!

She keeps daily journals on the newborns until the day she turns them over to CCI. The eight-week-old puppies are then assigned to volunteers all over the country. Cathy sends the puppy raisers copies of the journal and dozens of pictures.

New volunteers and staff at CCI are bowled over by Cathy's enthusiasm and willingness to do the impossible. Recently, and in secret, friends and admirers joined forces to turn an impossible dream into reality. They nominated Cathy Phillips to carry the 2002 Olympic torch as it wound its way through southern California and on to Salt Lake City. "Running the Olympic torch was the most incredible moment of my life!" she says. "I knew it would be awesome. I had no idea of the totally overwhelming, wonderful feeling it would be."

More than 100 CCI volunteers congregated along the torch run in Laguna Beach and cheered as Cathy ran by. The torch was bright; Cathy's smile was glowing. "There were CCI people and dogs everywhere," Cathy remembers. "It's a day that will be with me forever."

The sting is still there, and always will be, when she talks about the life she lost. "Will I always miss them? You bet. But if their spirits are looking down at me, and I believe they are, I want to make them proud."

LOVE HEELS · Tales from Canine Companions for Independence

Puppy Raisers

Raising a CCI puppy is like walking around with a rainbow over your head and a pot of gold at the end of the leash.

Puppy Raisers When a puppy is eight weeks old, the breeder caretaker turns it over to a puppy raiser to be trained and socialized for a period of thirteen to fifteen months. The puppy raisers are all volunteers. At the end of that time, the puppies are returned to Canine Companions for Independence for six months of advanced training.

ozzie
Gentle Giant

It's the truth, the whole scoop, and nothing but the poop, so help him God. Really. Promise. Trust me, the young boy vowed. Eleven-year-old Thomas Stanworth sat his parents down and outlined his reasons for getting what he wanted. His arguments made sense; but more than that, they made his parents proud.

Thomas was campaigning to adopt and raise a service dog over the next sixteen months. He needed his parents' consent to apply for a Canine Companion for Independence, and he swore to them that he would do the work. Especially the poop patrol.

His introduction to the world of service dog training had begun early in his fifth year of school. His teacher, Ms. Laura Bowen, had signed on as a puppy raiser for the same service organization and had brought her trainee to class. The puppy, a Labrador/golden retriever mix named Kiana, had been no bigger than a football.

"There are many things in life that will catch your eye, but only a few that will catch your heart ... pursue those." —Anonymous

As fall turned into winter, the little Lab grew along with Thomas's interest in the program. He understood all that his teacher told him about helping others, and that these dogs would help people with physical disabilities live more independent lives. The thought intrigued him. He didn't really know anyone who used a wheelchair to get around. He knew there were some kids at his school in wheelchairs, but he never had either the reason or the chance to get to know them.

Thomas grew especially close to Kiana; she listened to him and did what he asked. He learned to be firm and consistent, and it was that lesson that convinced

ozzie

Thomas's parents that he was up to the challenge. He swore he'd clean up after the dog, and exercise and train it, too. He even offered to pay for the dog's food from his allowance. His parents outlined several reasons for saying no. They were especially worried that the young boy's heart would break when it came time to give the puppy back. They even offered to buy him a purebred Lab of his own. He declined, insisting that raising a service dog was better. In the end, Curt and Terri Stanworth finally agreed. Both figured it would be months before their son's new puppy would arrive, plenty of time for him to lose interest and change his mind.

But Thomas's new charge arrived at the Southwest Regional Center in Oceanside, California, within the month. Puppy program assistant Val Valentine met the family in the lobby with a beautiful, well-mannered puppy. It was not big, not especially small, and the best part was how well it listened. Terri Stanworth relaxed, thinking it was going to be fun to raise this little dog. Mother and son signed the papers, watched a video about the CCI program, and signed up for training lessons. When it was time to leave with their new charge, Terri picked up the leash and waited for Valentine to say thank you.

But when Valentine returned to the room, she wasn't alone. Valentine put a squirmy white puppy with an extremely large head into Thomas's arms. Then the introductions: "Thomas," she said, "this is Osmond, officially known as Osmond II."

Huh?

Turned out the well-trained pooch at Terri's feet was Valentine's own puppy-in-training, a little retriever named Cinders.

Oops.

Thomas turned his nose up at the name Osmond and asked, "Suppose I called him Ozzie, would that be okay?" Thomas walked out of the center with a big

smile on his face, one matched only in intensity by the wiggle of Ozzie's whole backside. They looked right together; the world looked right when they were together.

The little boy and the little dog drew admiration from passersby. But the dog didn't stay little for long and neither did the boy. Both had spurts of growth, competing in pounds and inches.

The two settled into a routine. Ozzie stayed home with Terri while Thomas went to school. The dog always met Thomas at the door, waiting there minutes before the boy walked in. He sat at the boy's feet until his homework was done, and then it was time either for dog training, throwing the ball, or snuggling in front of the TV. If Ozzie had been taught to use the remote control, the TV would have been permanently tuned to *Animal Planet*. The dog raced to the screen to get a closer sniff of lions and tigers and bears.

Ozzie had a favorite blanket and a favorite spot—anywhere next to Thomas. Even at bedtime, the two were inseparable, and that was okay with the boy.

The months passed and the puppy kept growing: seventy pounds, eighty pounds, eighty-five, eighty-six. When it looked as if a talking scale would grunt, "One at a time, please," Ozzie was put on a diet. He scaled back to a sleek seventy-two pounds on a diet of low-calorie food and string beans.

The dog grew too big to share Thomas's bed, so he bunked next to the boy on the floor. He'd steal the blanket off the bed and wrap his body around it, a habit he'd picked up as a pup.

Training came easily to the boy and the dog. Puppy-school classmates were astounded as they watched the boy handle the huge dog with the confidence of a pro. Ozzie, who almost always walked on a loose lead, sat, stayed, and followed Thomas with adoring eyes. Except when they passed candy counters that begged to be sniffed or the dog-food aisle at the market. Meat counters were tough to ignore, too.

The dog made the boy laugh, especially in the late evening when Thomas's dad would light a fire in the family room. Dad settled in a soft recliner; Ozzie snuggled by the fire. Let the countdown begin—five, four, three, two, one. Like clockwork, a symphony of deafening snores would begin, chasing the rest of the family away. The dog has since outgrown the need to snore; Dad hasn't.

The months have dwindled into just weeks and days before the two must part. Terri watches her son come to grips with reality, and she says he amazes her with his unselfishness and maturity.

Ozzie needs a job; he likes to work, Thomas tells people who ask about the future. He's more than just a pet, and Thomas promises to find him a job helping people if he doesn't make the CCI cut.

And what will Ozzie tell his new owner? Ozzie likes to go to the movies, eats slowly, and will do anything you tell him to do for a green bean treat.

Yes, Ozzie's head is big, and sometimes people say he looks like a white Saint Bernard, but he's the gentlest of giants. Ozzie, Thomas says, was born to love and be loved.

EPILOGUE: In November 2002, Ozzie graduated as a facility dog and was placed with teaching assistant Peggy Solis and principal Lee Anderson at the California Avenue School in southern California. The public school serves more than 300 special needs children.

The Long Goodbye

Adam Afflalo's small, battered body was covered with cuts and bruises. One broken leg hung suspended from a metal-and-cloth cradle while a half dozen machines wheezed and sputtered in the small room at Children's Hospital in San Diego, California.

A service dog was sitting by his bed. A huge, gentle dog, dressed in a yellow cape with blue trim. Adam reached down and grabbed the dog's right ear, squeezing it tight to make his own pain go away. The dog didn't pull back or growl. Instead, he offered a paw. The two stared into each other's eyes. The dog licked the boy's hand; the boy sobbed.

"Truly, it is in the darkness that one finds the light, so when we are in sorrow, then this light is nearest of all to us." —Meister Eckhart

Eleven-year-old Adam had just been told that his twelve-year-old sister, Aleszondra, had died in the same accident that had left his body badly broken. The two children had been hit by a car in a crosswalk on their way to school. Adam didn't let go of Icon's paw for a long while; Icon didn't move, either.

❤

Icon II is a Canine Companions for Independence (CCI) puppy-in-training, a golden retriever/Labrador mix, and I am his trainer. But just for another two days. Then he goes to canine college and will be out of my life for six months. The separation is necessary to break our bond. I can't even pack him a bag with treats and toys, something to remember me by. I have been asked to return Icon wearing his brass ID tag, yellow cape, and one unwrapped nylon bone. It was always supposed to

No one is supposed to touch a CCI dog without permission while he or she is training, and that's been the hardest part of my job as his teacher.

be this way. Icon was born with a job waiting for him to grow into, and it's time. He'll learn dozens of skills so he can, literally, open doors for people with disabilities.

Icon's visit with Adam wasn't the first time the CCI dog helped someone. He's been there for lots of hurts, some of them mine. And there's a big hurt heading my way. But I knew there was an end right from the beginning. I just wonder, where has all our time together gone in the last year? But oh, the adventures the two of us have had along the way! Some amusing, others heartfelt. Some sad.

♥

No one is supposed to touch a CCI dog without permission while he or she is training, and that's been the hardest part of my job as his teacher. Everything about Icon makes people want to touch and hug him—from his soft, golden coat to his doe-like eyes. We've been lots of places—Mass on Sundays, fast-food and fancy restaurants, casual parties and black-tie affairs. And we've spent more than a few Friday nights at the movies. Summer nights meant Balboa Park for museums and Old Globe plays. Or trolley trips to the Navy Pier downtown to hear the San Diego Symphony's Summer Pops.

But it hasn't been all play and no work. In my job as a newspaper reporter, we've covered press confer-

ences, lots of them. That January day when Icon and Adam Afflalo met in the boy's hospital room, we were covering a press conference in the hospital garden. On another occasion, when he was much younger, Icon shamed a long-winded admiral into cutting his speech short with a loud, doggie yawn. After that, Icon learned to sit quietly for hours at city council and county board meetings. Then back to the office, where Icon obediently sat under my desk while I filed my stories.

There have been embarrassing moments, such as the week before Christmas while shopping at a department store. I was in a h-u-r-r-y—a word I have learned to spell and not speak. You see, "hurry" in CCI lingo means toilet. Potty. Pee now, please. On this particular day, I was in a hurry and Icon wanted to ramble. "Hurry," I commanded. And so he stopped and squatted. I have always carried an emergency backpack filled with paper towels, scoop bags, a plastic bottle filled with antibacterial soap, floral spray, and bribes—uh, treats. I cleaned up his mess. Then I apologized to Icon and thanked him for being so obedient.

Raising a CCI puppy is like walking around with a rainbow over your head and a pot of gold at the end of the leash. And so I've signed on, again. Icon and I recently drove to Lindbergh Field to pick up three golden retriever/Labrador mix puppies to take to CCI's regional center in Oceanside. One would be mine to raise, but I had not yet been told which. One crate held a shy male. No amount of verbal soothing consoled him. A second crate held two furry dynamos, a male and a female. One barked a lot; the other was quietly insistent. Pushy. I put the two crates in the back of my Jeep and put Icon in the middle. One puppy settled into a nap less than a mile from the airport. The second yapped for most of the forty-five-minute drive; the third hogged most of the front of the crate.

I wondered which was mine, which lesson I had unconsciously decided to bring into my life. The shy puppy who needed lots of reassurance? The one who never shut up? The pushy one? Yep, mine's the pushy one, Hiley. The two of us have a lot of teaching and learning to do over the next year. Having Hiley doesn't make losing Icon less painful. I know I have taught Icon as much as I can, and now it's up to the professional trainers at CCI. But truthfully, I'm finding it hard to let him go.

Icon was born February 24, 1998, the third puppy in a litter of eight, and the butterball of the lot. His face was different from those of his siblings; more Lab than golden, according to Susan Amidon. The Amidons—Susan, husband Norman, and their two young sons, Scott and David—volunteered to be a breeder-caretaker family. That's how they got Elsie, Icon's mom.

Eight weeks came and went. Time to turn the litter back to CCI so each could get a checkup, tattoo, and name. Then on to their very own puppy raisers. Qualified homes were found for all but two puppies, one being Icon. Susan Amidon agreed to foster both puppies for a short time. The other left after a week, but not Icon. A couple of weeks later, he was flown to CCI's Oceanside center with the hope that he would find a home. While the search continued, veteran CCI puppy raisers Mike and Sue Calvert agreed to fill in the gap. A week or two, they thought. But weeks turned into months. And it was impossible to find anyone to take Icon even for a getaway weekend because he was still having accidents inside their home. Nobody wanted a dog that wasn't housebroken. "But, of all the puppies I've loved and raised, this one had that something special," Sue Calvert said. "I could see it in his eyes and feel it in my heart." A big part of her wanted to keep Icon for the next year. But the Calvert household already had two family dogs, three cats, and a CCI puppy who would stay for another six months. Sue dreaded the thought of not having Icon. But she knew it would be best for him to have a puppy raiser all to himself. "This is a program that revolves around putting others first; it's not about us," she said. "It's about what's best for the dogs, to help them graduate and go on to help people with disabilities enjoy more independent lives."

It became clear as the Fourth of July came and went that Icon needed more than the Calverts could give him. But who would take a five-month-old puppy that was not completely toilet trained?

I liked the idea of raising puppies. I'd done it a couple of times before and never minded the sleepless nights and midnight cries. But every pet person has that one special, furry friend that never leaves the heart. For me, it will always be Shadow, a sixty-six-pound Lab mix who was mine from the day I spotted her nose poking out of a wire fence at the Humane

icon

Society's kennels on Sherman Street. She died of old age a couple of years ago. My eyes always seem to scan the crowd looking for black Labs, and Shadow had been on my mind a lot since I had decided to find another dog shortly after the Fourth of July. Less than a week later, I spotted Shadow's doggy double while I was with friends at a downtown seafood eatery. I couldn't take my eyes off her, even though it made my heart ache. But this dog was different. She wore a blue cape and sat quietly under a table at the feet of a young boy in a wheelchair. I studied the blue-and-yellow logo stitched on her cape: Canine Companions for Independence. I looked them up in the phone book when I got home. I wanted to raise a black Lab, and it had to be a female.

❤

The application came in the mail a few days later. I filled it out that same evening, put a stamp on the

Icon's eyes are like two saucers filled with black java. Decaf when you need to wind down, and the leaded stuff when you need a jolt of energy.

envelope, and walked to the corner mailbox. The next day, I telephoned to find out how soon I could have my puppy. It was a Tuesday morning in mid-July when my final at-home interview was scheduled. I dusted and vacuumed. Southwest CCI puppy program manager Jeanie Clark took one look at my tile floor and smiled. I thought I had scored bonus points for my good housekeeping.

We talked for over an hour about my thoughts, experiences, and philosophy on raising a puppy; about CCI and its mission. I liked what I heard, and apparently she liked what she saw. Clark asked me to join their program and accept a puppy. That's when I placed my order: a black Lab, female. I think I said "please" when I finished my list of demands. Her face fell. She confessed that she'd had another puppy in mind, a male Lab mix who had been in foster care and desperately needed a home because he was coming up on five months old. Nope, I told her. Make mine eight weeks, female and black. When the words "just like Shadow" came out of my mouth, a light bulb went on in my head. "This whole thing, this puppy program, it's not about me, is it?" I said. "Could we start this interview all over again?" I asked. "Please?"

Four days later in Oceanside, Clark's office door opened and a forty-pound bundle of golden energy bounced into the room and landed smack in my heart. Icon's wiggly body said "puppy," though he was a mix of playful and prudent. Icon's eyes are like two saucers filled with black java. Decaf when you need to wind down, and the leaded stuff when you need a jolt of energy. In the time that I've had him, Icon has worked his way into many hearts. My seven-year-old nephew, Cole Van Middlesworth, has helped with the training, even though Icon outweighs him by a third. Each has learned to listen to the other and has taken turns leading and following. "I think Icon makes people feel happy. People who don't even know each other start talking and smiling when Icon is around," Cole said. "He's a very, very, good boy, and I'm going to be sad when he goes away."

♥

Dogs are dogs, and I'm not one to give them people skills. Still, I wonder, if the two of us could have a last conversation before Saturday afternoon, what would Icon say to console me?

There's no doubt in my heart that he would do just that; he was born and bred to nurture. Six months from now, we'll meet again. That's when he'll graduate from advanced training and get a new owner. I've watched the ceremony twice before with Icon securely tucked beneath my chair. Puppy raisers hand over their canine charges with one hand and wipe the tears from their eyes with the other. Hardly anybody ever looks back. Saturday is Icon's turn. And mine.

"How can you bear to give him away?" so many people asked me all along the road from July to May. "He's not my dog," I would tell them, really believing that during much of our time together. But Icon *is* my dog, and when we are no longer a team, when my part ends on Saturday, a big part of my heart will go along with him.

EPILOGUE: After two years of growing and learning, Icon was paired with his very own person, nineteen-year-old college student Abram Bryson, who lives in Utah. Abram and Icon have formed a very special bond since they were teamed, and that silly grin on Icon's face says it all. Finally, my sweet boy has his very own person to love unconditionally and to be loved by in return.

Take care of each other,
Icon's mom (Patricia Dibsie)

Freedom Endures

It was a grand old day, a flag-waving day, and most of the townspeople in Colorado Springs, Colorado, had lined the streets to celebrate. They put on the red, white, and blue, waved Old Glory, and made much ado over the little black Lab.

He had been in town only a few weeks before the Fourth of July. The date was circled on the kitchen calendar, and the words "picnic and parade" were scribbled in red ink. The morning of the Fourth, Sue and Dave Calvano tied a blue-and-yellow cape around the puppy's chest along with a patriotic neck scarf. After a short car ride, the trio arrived at the designated spot.

"We must accept finite disappointment, but we must never lose infinite hope." —Martin Luther King Jr.

His new puppy raisers scooped him up and plopped him down on soft bales of hay, stacked especially high since he was the guest of honor. The rolling platform surged forward—a float, he'd heard them call it—and slowly made its way down the town's main street. The people waved and screamed his name. They had all come to celebrate Freedom, which was the little dog's name.

Months of growing and learning lay ahead, but today was just for play; everything was in honor of Freedom. Some welcoming party! They embraced Freedom as if he were the most important puppy on earth.

The Calvanos laughed whenever they called his name. Friends laughed, people hugged when they said his name. And so he figured that Freedom must be a very, very good name. Besides the smiles on the people's faces, there always seemed to be treats in their hands. Answering the call to Freedom was going to be a very, very good thing.

July passed and the puppy grew. August came and went. It was hot and long, but not much else happened. Freedom learned to sit and stay and toilet on command. His body tripled in size as it grew into his gigantic paws.

When September came, the children moaned. Summer was over and everyone began to settle into a comfortable working rhythm. And then, eleven days into September, the name that had once brought so much joy to so many didn't work anymore. In fact, his name began to make almost everyone teary. Nothing much made sense. One moment life was one way; a moment later it was the other.

Sue Calvano was driving to her office when she heard the terrible, unbelievable news. She grabbed Freedom and sobbed, using his shiny coat to mop up her tears. She shook her head, pulled her car to the side of the road, and turned the radio volume up. The voices Freedom heard screaming from the dashboard radio were panicky, stirring fear into his owner's heart. Something was very, very wrong.

Freedom was silenced.

They pulled into the parking lot and ran into the building. People everywhere were sobbing and telling one another that it just wasn't so. They collected in groups, surrounding the few television sets that lined their office walls.

Freedom was being put to the test.

An airplane had plowed into the World Trade Center in New York City. So much smoke and fire, so many lives lost. And this was just the beginning. Within minutes, a second plane hit the adjoining tower, and within an hour both lay in rubble.

Freedom came with a price tag in human suffering and loss.

After September 11, nothing was the same. Now, when anyone spoke his name, it took on a whole new meaning. In the days that followed, people from all over the building wandered down to visit Freedom. They said they needed to stroke and hug him; people needed to embrace Freedom. Life was a little less secure, and it made Sue's world feel a little more sane when she could look down and see Freedom at her feet. She would stroke him and whisper his name, reminding herself that Freedom takes care and work. Nothing worthwhile is free or easy or always safe. People had died, and America's military were ready to put their lives on the line for Freedom.

Freedom endures.

Freedom and Sue took their first post-9/11 airplane trip to San Diego after the first of the year. She remembers feeling safe with Freedom at her side. Security officers searched Sue's baggage and waved her through the metal detector, Freedom trotting along beside her. His bag, brimming with toys and treats, brought laughs. They headed for the departure gate, followed by laughs and claps from onlookers when Sue called his name. Even the army reservists on duty smiled and nodded.

Freedom reigns.

Of Loss and Love

orantes

As a breeder caretaker and puppy raiser, Annie Williams has nurtured many CCI dogs. Shown here, from left to right, are Orantes, Woosley, Carole II, and Alfre.

The plane was small, noisy, and, worst of all, running late. Perched behind a line of a dozen metal birds, the twelve-seater waited its turn to take wing and ride the wind. Annie Williams tightened her seatbelt, a reflex action that belied her outward appearance of composure. She glanced at the man strapped into the aisle seat next to her. Their elbows dueled for position on the small armrest, and a truce was sealed with a smile.

As Annie crossed and uncrossed her ankles, her mind skipped from the deep sorrows of yesterdays to the promises of years of tomorrows and back again. Mostly, her thoughts were of Lane. They were always focused on Lane when she was forced to sit and be still. Her only son had been killed in an automobile accident nearly two years ago. The two years ago had stretched into forever ago, but the pain was as piercing as the day she lost Lane.

Something stirred at her feet.

Annie pictured her son's smile, replayed his boisterous laughs, and remembered his love of all things animal.

"Each new season grows from the leftovers of the past. That is the essence of change, and change is the essence of life." —Hal Borland

Again, something stirred at her feet. Annie was traveling with Orantes, a golden retriever/Labrador mix. The caped Canine Companion-in-training was tuned into Annie's mood and nudged her to offer comfort. Annie gave Orantes a scratch behind both ears, and memories of Lane tugged her back to her son's childhood. There was always an animal or two in the home; always had been since Annie was a child. But with Lane it was different; with him, the animals were more people than pets. He had had a way of understanding, a way of knowing and bonding with animals that had never ceased to amaze her. And he taught her about being with animals in a way that was different from any experience in her own childhood.

Meanwhile, the plane lurched forward to take a position closer to the jumping-off point on the runway. Annie settled back, and her mind reached into the past. She chuckled out loud. Funny, she thought, parents were the ones who taught children, but in her life it had been so much the other way around. Funny.

The plane pitched forward a third, a fourth time, and more times that she could keep track of. Then a rumbling preceded a roar that catapulted her mind and body back to the present. Frightened, she turned her head to look at the Armani-clad businessman to her left. He looked different. He had a furry thing wrapped around his shoulders. Later, Annie would confess that she remembered thinking how odd it was that the man had a dog on his lap.

Oops. Orantes had crawled up on the man's lap, planted her paws on his thick shoulder pads, and nudged her nose into his neck. The expression on her face was a sorry mixture of giddiness and guffaw. The man had put his arms around Orantes, comforting the dog as if it were a frightened child. And then he turned his attention to Annie and offered her the same measure of reassurance.

Recalling this incident when both she and Orantes feared for their lives, Annie blushes as she recounts her earliest experiences as a puppy raiser. First-time puppy

raisers have a bible full of humbling parables to share, often with lessons much like those in the Good Book.

It takes time and seasoning to be able to laugh at your own mistakes. Annie has put in the time and appreciates a good laugh, even at her own expense. She's raising dog number eight, Zaret, which pretty much takes her from A to Z. Then there are the "grandkids."

In addition to raising puppies, Annie took on the role of breeder caretaker when she accepted Carole, a breeder dog, into her home. Canine Companions selects a handful of top dogs to provide quality puppies for the program. Carole has produced twenty-seven puppies, many of which have been placed with disabled partners. Her last litter of eight has now been trained, and the dogs have been paired with partners.

Part of Annie's involvement in Canine Companions is to honor her son's love of animals and to pass on all that he taught her. This puppy raiser, breeder caretaker, major fundraiser, donor, and CCI ambassador is too modest to count the ways she makes a difference in the lives of people and animals.

So let me sing her praises, joined by a choir of friends and furry fans:

We salute you, Annie, and thank you, those of us from Carole's last "A" litter. You taught our little ones to trust and be happy during those first formative days and weeks. Day and night we made demands on you, and you always answered our cries.

Love and puppy licks,
Alfre, Angelo, Armani, Acton,
Andrew, Autumn, Agar, and Axel

Ten Ways to Recognize a CCI Puppy Raiser

1. They embrace the fashion statement "NO outfit is complete without dog hair."

2. They can produce a plastic poop bag from thin air, then stoop and scoop in a single bound.

3. They never use the word "hurry" when they're in a rush; it means "squat."

4. They can snip nails on a moving target with PAWSitive results.

5. When they think of a treat, liver chips and peanut-butter biscuits top the list.

6. To quiet loud and mouthing puppies, they spray them sparingly with their favorite perfume, eau de vinegar. Puppies, however, prefer plain toilet water.

7. They have a puppy under their desk at work and underfoot at home.

8. They have a long list of "most embarrassing moments," but speak of them with humility, not humiliation.

9. They raise miracles one puppy at a time.

10. No matter how stoic they may be, they all need a box of tissues when the time comes to say goodbye and send their puppies off to college.

heather
Camp Anytown

The destination was any town, but not just any town would do. This particular "any town," a camp with a crusade, was located high on Palomar Mountain in San Diego County.

There was no boating scheduled at Camp Anytown; no hikes or archery lessons either. Campfires and camp food, yes; but the rest would all be new to a busload of junior and senior high school students who had come up from the city. Scary stories were told around late-night campfires, and these tales were especially scary because the teens talked honestly about their feelings.

This camp's overriding mission was to teach teens to identify and eliminate feelings of bias, bigotry, and racism. These particular kids came from different economic and religious backgrounds. Some were tall, others were short; some were fat, others were skinny; and they came in all shades—black, white, yellow, and brown.

"The most important single ingredient in the formula of success is knowing how to get along with people." —Theodore Roosevelt

When the bus pulled up to camp early on a Friday morning, the first thing the kids spotted was a dog sniffing around their bags. Word traveled that it was a drug dog, so no one came near it or offered it a friendly pat on the head. It was going to be that kind of weekend, kids versus adults, they figured. No trust here, they whispered to one another.

Willie Crawford, the camp counselor, stood on the sidelines and watched as the kids grabbed their bags and headed for their assigned dorms. Funny, she remembers thinking, none of these kids warmed up to her dog. She had brought Heather, a six-month-old service dog trainee, to help break the ice with the teens. But, if anything, Heather's presence had the opposite effect.

Later, Willie and Heather took their seats at the lunch table and watched as kids filled every seat but the ones next to them. The tables filled up fast, and late-comers were forced to take the only empty seats, near Willie and Heather. The counselor introduced Heather and talked about her training as a service dog.

The teens laughed and confessed that they thought her dog was a drug dog. That explains every-thing, Willie said to herself. The kids were about to learn a lesson about jumping to conclusions. The Canine Companion for Independence puppy had barely begun her own lessons when she was thrust into the role of teacher.

And so she taught them, and very well. Heather turned out to be the perfect weekend icebreaker. Heather, a Fourth of July puppy, represented free-dom that January weekend. She opened dialogue about other assumptions the kids had made about life.

Heather spent much of the weekend sitting quiet-ly by Willie's side. Just having her there at camp, the kids told the counselor, made them feel more com-fortable and less judged. At the end of the day, Willie

would take off Heather's blue-and-gold cape and allow her to play. The kids were surprised at how nuts the dog would go when work was over. She loved to explore, play ball, chase and be chased. Later, she would want to cud-dle. One girl, who confessed to a fear of dogs, got up the nerve to call Heather over to her. Brave, the other girls called her, and then the con-versation turned to things the others feared.

The last night, at the candlelight ceremony, the teens talked about what they had learned. One of the first kids to take the candle and speak thanked Heather for the difference she had made by just being there. He told the others it was one of his first times away from home and that he had felt very frightened until he spotted the puppy. Heather sat adoringly at his side with her chin on his leg.

No one comes out of this camp unchanged after taking the time to understand and care about other people, Willie said. Many of the teens admitted that the experience was the first time they had dared to talk so openly and honestly about what they needed from other kids. And, in turn, had taken the time to listen to what others needed from them. They learned to build an inclusive community, one that gave everyone equal opportunities and respect, including the physically challenged.

The teens were given a firsthand experience in the challenges of being disabled during a luncheon exer-cise. Some teens were blindfolded, some were given earplugs to wear, and others were confined to chairs. A few teens were told they couldn't speak; some had an arm tied behind their backs.

The isolation was incredible, some complained. The everyday tasks involved in eating lunch turned from easy to nearly impossible. Frustration erupted. Then self-examination, a little guilt at taking so much for granted, then brainstorming for ways to even the playing field for the physically challenged. The kids came to understand how a service dog could make impossible tasks possible. They thought about the difficulty of doing the everyday things, which had never occurred to them before this experience, and left the mess hall with their eyes opened.

And their hearts, too, thanks to a little yellow Lab named Heather.

Passing the Buck

blanche

The man didn't like dealing with banks; didn't like checkbooks or plastic cards. The first of every month, he counted out five hundred-dollar bills and put them in his landlord's hand.

Except this once, when nobody was home and he was in a hurry to catch the bus for work. Couldn't hurt to slip the bills under the door, he figured. The landlord would know it was from him. He recounted the bills and smoothed them on his shirt, using his palm as an iron. Then he slipped the notes under the door.

Neat.

"The really happy man is one who can enjoy the scenery on a detour." —Anonymous

But something went wrong on the locked side of the door. The bills didn't stay put. Swiped. Gone. He got down on his knees and peered through the crack at the bottom of the door. Nothing.

The man ran home, made a 911 call to his landlord, and told his story to the answering machine. He swore he'd put the bills under the door; paid up the first, as he had every other month. But someone or something on the other side of the door had made off with the loot.

Swear to God, he said in a panicked voice.

♥

The number 3 was blinking on the answering machine when Rick and Bonnie Mueller returned home from a twenty-nine-minute trip to the market. The first two calls were from friends who wanted nothing in particular, just to say a quick hello.

The third call stopped them cold. The voice was panicky and the words too rushed to make sense. They knew it was Roger and that he was upset, rambling on about "money," "rent," and "gone."

They played the tape back, finally understood the message, then turned to stare at Blanche.

♥

If dogs could shrug and play innocent, Blanche's performance would have been considered flawless. As dogs go, Blanche was, well, Blanche was gorgeous. She had that "Who, me?" look about her, grinning and trying to engage the couple in a game of ball.

If dogs could talk, Blanche would have told them about the bills. Nice treat for leaving me alone, she would have reasoned. Not as good as liver or cheese, but paper is fun to chew. A new kind of game. Who knew?

But dogs can't look innocent and dogs can't talk. She surrendered to a "down" position and watched her favorite people head toward her den to reclaim her new paper toys.

They reclaimed two untouched Benjamin Franklin bills and two more with lots of teeth marks and tears. Tatters of green confetti were sprinkled at the back of Blanche's kennel, and, on closer inspection, bits of green paper were caught in her back teeth.

The prosecution rests. Guilty.

No, not the dog. Rick and Bonnie. The seasoned puppy raisers were guilty of misjudgment. They thought that Blanche, at eight months, was ready for her first "home alone" trial run. Turned out they were wrong, and the penalty was going to stink.

Blanche was sent to bed on a full stomach. Rick and Bonnie would have to wait until morning to reclaim bits and pieces of their missing money. Nothing more could be done until Blanche passed the buck.

Next morning, right as rain, Blanche gobbled her breakfast and brought her leash to Rick for their morning ritual. She sniffed in her usual spot, squatted, and got down to business. Her poop was brown and solid, dotted with green confetti. Rick scooped the poop and picked out the paper with a plastic knife and fork. Bonnie washed and dried the Franklin flecks, and then the two sat down to put the $100 puzzle back together again. The picture revealed the serial number and most of Franklin's face. They taped their prize together, and then Bonnie went in search of a bank that would pay them for their trouble.

The woman at the first bank listened as Bonnie told her tale, Blanche sitting dutifully at her side. The teller nodded as the story unfolded and rendered a one-word verdict: Sorry. The two were off to a second bank, where Bonnie retold the story. This time she had Blanche perform an "up" command so she could look the teller in the eyes. It worked. But then, Bonnie says, almost everything seems to work with Blanche at her side.

gold
The Learning Curve

Linda Dreyfuss has survived cancer, thrives on challenges, and believes that almost anything is possible with the right mix of puppies and pupils. And that, the second-grade teacher from San Diego smiles, is how she came to learn one of life's greatest lessons. It didn't come fast, or easy, but nothing worthwhile comes fast or easy. She knows that now, thanks to three puppies. And, she's happy to report, her pupils are beginning to figure that out for themselves at a very young age.

Kids and puppies, and adults, too, are what they are and must be nurtured to bring out the best of whatever's there. Affection and acceptance, patience and prodding, those are her golden rules.

And that brings this story to Grover, a wide-eyed, four-legged juvenile delinquent who found trouble as easily as a hound sniffs out the fox. And he made about as much noise in the process.

"The most important thing I have learned over the years is the difference between taking one's work seriously and taking one's self seriously. The first is imperative; the second is disastrous." —Margaret Fontey

Grover, a Canine Companion for Independence puppy, was Linda's first charge. She had high hopes for the golden retriever from the moment he was placed in her hands. Innocent and curious, the puppy was no bigger than a breadbox. But, no matter how you sliced it, this was no working dog. It took Grover fourteen months to convince her, but in the end it was Linda who cried uncle.

She remembers feeling that she had failed him. But that was then and now is

Gold was small enough for the kids to hold when he first came to

now. She understands that Grover was never CCI material. He didn't like following orders, didn't like sitting still for more than a minute, and never saw a ball he didn't want to chase. When he didn't get his own way, he pitched a fit that grew more intense with every passing month.

When Grover was released from CCI, Linda placed him with a family as a pet. He lives on a big ranch and, at age three, hasn't mellowed one bit. His new family loves his spunk and makes sure he gets lots of exercise.

It was a happy ending for Grover; not so for Linda. She was determined to raise another puppy. And this time, she swore, she was going to do it right. She laughs about that now; there wasn't any right or wrong with Grover. But that was something Gobi was going to have to teach her.

♥

Lesson One: You can't force a square peg into a round hole.

Gobi, a petite, purebred Labrador retriever, was four months old when she was teamed with Linda. More white than yellow, Gobi drew stares wherever she pranced. The puppy listened and obviously adored Linda; her brown eyes tracked her trainer's every move. Linda felt redeemed. She could hold her head up high when she took Gobi to puppy classes.

Gobi thrived in advanced training and was placed as a skilled companion. Give that girl a gold star!

♥

Lesson Two: You can't take a whole lot of credit when a square peg fits into a square hole.

Then came Gold, black Gold. No Texas tea for him, thank you; Gold would rather gulp life than sip it. But he's smooth, if you overlook his tendency to take things that don't belong to him. Linda blames it

on his passive need for attention. It comes out in the form of taking things that aren't his, she says, objecting to the word "stealing."

The Lab is her golden boy, just a kid who wants attention when Mom is on the phone. After school, when all the kids have gone home and Linda's attention is focused on grading papers, Gold scours the floor looking for tidbits of leftover lunch. Next, Gold sticks his nose where it doesn't belong—in the kids' desks, looking for pink erasers to chomp.

But the kids forgive him; they gladly trade a few rubber stubs for the pleasure of his company. Chelsea says she loves him, especially during independent reading. She finds it soothing; it's easier to concentrate when she's stroking Gold. Reading out loud comes easier for others; they tell Linda it keeps them from being nervous.

When Bobby and Jerald tackle difficult math problems, they sit on the floor with Gold between them. Bobby says Gold can tell when they get frustrated; he licks them. It makes them laugh, and then they go back to work and start over. The rule is that Gold can stay only if the kids keep working. That and NO LICKING! But then who's snitching!

Gold was small enough for the kids to hold when he first came to class; now the kids have a tough time holding their own. Gold weighs more than most of the second graders and is going through doggy adolescence. The kids are learning to be firm but gentle. Kind of like what their teacher does with them, they've noticed.

Although Gold is still a work in progress, he has taught Linda well.

♥

Lesson Three: Take your work seriously; not yourself. Life's too short. 🐴

class; now the kids have a tough time holding their own.

All My Children

flynn dogs

Like the battery bunny, the Flynn family just keeps on going and growing, one miracle puppy at a time. The firefighter and his high school sweetheart sent their tenth puppy off to college and welcomed number eleven.

And yes, there were tears, always tears. Typical parents, their watery eyes reveal a mixture of grief and gratitude as they proudly watch their "canine children" graduate to the next stage of life. "You shed a few tears, but you soak up the tears with a fluffy eight-week-old puppy," says Captain Dan Flynn, a California firefighter. "When you have kids, you don't plan on them staying with you all of your life. They grow up, get married, and you end up with a bigger family."

Janice Flynn has chronicled their puppy family's growth in words and pictures that say volumes about their years of experience. Some of their puppies have graduated to become Canine Companions; some have been released and placed in loving homes. Whatever the career path, the Flynns embrace their dogs' new partners, spouses, children, siblings, and in-laws.

"Each friend represents a world in us, a world possibly not born until they arrive, and it is only by this meeting that a new world is born." —Anaïs Nin

The good news just keeps multiplying. Vacations often include visits to their newly acquired family members for reunions, college graduations, birthdays, and even, in one case, a wedding. "You never stop loving your puppy, and it's important for us to know that they're happy and healthy," Janice says. "The bonus has been meeting our dogs' new families and becoming a part of their lives, too."

Their canine family began with Gable, a male Labrador retriever who skipped a semester in college and was placed with Californian Rita Roberson. Gable was loved, perhaps more than most, or maybe it was because he was the first. First times are the hardest; it was for the Flynns, and they watch as others go through the same trauma.

The Flynns wanted the world for Gable; Roberson needed Gable to offer her a world of independence. Cerebral palsy had robbed her body of the ability to do the simple things in life and made every move a challenge. "Rita spent time at a center for persons with disabilities, helping with computers," Janice says. "Once a month I would meet her there to pick up Gable and groom him for her. We got to know one another through Gable, and a friendship grew."

Meanwhile, the Flynns were busy grooming their second dog for a companion career. Muriel was a small black Labrador who was as sweet as she was smart. The Flynns liked training puppies and were impressed with both the program and the success of Canine Companions for Independence. "We were only going to raise one dog," Janice says. "After that, we thought we'd be ready for another pet of our own. But we got hooked. The dogs are amazing. We just stayed on and volunteered our time at CCI wherever it was needed."

Muriel grew in stature, stamina, and smarts. She was a natural, looking for ways to help Dan and Janice. They knew the day they gave her back that she would be graduating with a partner. Some dogs shine, and Muriel sparkled. She learned all of the service commands easily, but the trainers decided Muriel was best suited for work as a hearing dog. She was sent to the organization's Northeast Regional Center in New York for additional training and was placed with Lois

Hansen. The team of Muriel and Lois moved several times, eventually settling down in Washington State. The two blended and complemented each other. When someone wanted Hansen's attention, Muriel would sit at her feet to alert her. When doorbells, phones, and timers chimed, rang, and dinged, Muriel was off to get Lois.

Hansen's world opened up with Muriel beside her. She met "Mr. Right," courted, and walked down the aisle with Muriel at her side as "best dog." The Flynns attended the wedding. Dan was asked to read a poem as part of the ceremony. "We just felt like family," Janice says, adding, "We always do when we go up to visit."

The next Flynn dog, Reinert, was a male Labrador/golden retriever cross. He was a sweet dog but had some fears and insecurities that kept him from graduating. He was placed with California couple Dan and Diana Barnes. They own their own company, so they make the rules; Reinert goes to work with them most days, and that suits the Flynns just fine. "We met the Barneses at a parade," Janice says. "We were

walking down the street, and the minute they saw him they fell in love with him. They wanted to know all about CCI and how they could get involved. They attended some training classes and were thrilled when we asked them to puppy-sit Reinert."

When the dog was released, placing him with the Barneses was a natural. The couple put Reinert through therapy dog training school and took him to a convalescent home to visit Dan's mother several times a week. The visits were a huge success and added years to her life, the doctors told her son. She liked to think of Reinert as "her" dog and made sure everyone else knew that, too.

Then along came James, a yellow Labrador retriever who soared to the top of his training class under the Flynns' tutelage. Their reputation for turning out top dogs became legend.

Flynn dogs are known for their attention to detail. The Flynns' secret: hard work. They combed over the puppy-training manual twice before taking on their first charge. They practiced commands first with flash cards, then on each other, even before

once or twice a year to see them," Janice says. "We laugh a lot when we're with them. James has a great home, and Mary and David make us feel like part of the family, too."

Kilkenny came to the Flynns at eight months. CCI trainers were hoping that the Flynns could help the older puppy work out some serious behavior problems. But his aggression toward other dogs made it impossible for him to remain in the program. He was released and was adopted as a pet. The yellow Labrador has a happy life, playing on the beach, chasing balls, and loving his two new owners.

Kasten followed Kilkenny. The gorgeous female golden retriever was feisty, but definitely had all the makings of a Flynn dog. She brought Ruthie Rudek into the Flynn family. "Ruthie often comes down to stay with us, or we go up north to see her and

Flynn dogs—they don't come any better.

they brought home their first service dog. It has become a passion that has rubbed off on other puppy raisers, setting a higher standard and bumping the program up a notch. Flynn dogs—they don't come any better.

James graduated and was placed with Arizonan David Van Gorder. Van Gorder was a twenty-two-year-old construction worker when he fell from the roof of a house. He landed on his head, injuring his spine. He worked his way through anger and depression, then returned to school to build a new life and a new identity. Sixteen years later, Van Gorder graduated from college with a doctorate in psychology.

He met his future wife, Mary, at a mental health clinic where they both worked. She helped him with a lot of daily tasks until James came along and joined their family. Then Jimmy Joe, as David calls him, took over. "Dan and I really enjoy going to Arizona

Kasten," Janice says. Rudek lives with multiple sclerosis. "On good days, she can walk but needs Kasten in case she loses her balance." "They're a good match," Dan adds. "Ruthie is very much into computers and has given Kasten her own e-mail address, and includes lots of pictures of Kasten on her Web site." Dan says Kasten probably has racked up more frequent flier miles than any other CCI graduate, traveling with Ruthie to numerous destinations both in this country and abroad.

Presley moved in with the Flynns at the age of four months. But, like some Labs, Presley was no work and all play. He was released and was placed with people who adore him.

Shelton was their next puppy, a magnificent golden retriever who wanted to work from the moment he was given his first command, Janice remembers. "He would wait and watch for my words,

The Flynns

♥

janice & dan

★ gable

★ muriel

★ reinert

★ james

★ kasten

★ presley

★ shelton

★ romer

★ raive

★ kellin

then react immediately," she says. Yep, he went on to graduate and was partnered with Pete Wolcott, a high school science teacher who lives less than five miles from the Flynns. Janice is happy to pick up Shelton from school once a month to groom and love him. "We knew Pete before he was matched with Shelton," Janice says. "Dan and I were happily surprised when we learned that Shelton would be with Pete."

Romer, one of the most beautiful goldens ever to pass through CCI's doors, was shown the door after only a few months in advanced training. He retrieved beautifully and really enjoyed it, as well as performing a multitude of other tasks. There was one problem, though—he hated wearing his cape. Even as a puppy, Romer became a mutt on a mission once the jacket went on, rubbing his body against bushes, fences, trees, and walls. He also had some minor fears and handled stress poorly. But toy possession turned out to be his final undoing. Romer was downright selfish about his toys and was ready to take on any dog in defense of his property.

But Romer is stunning, and he knows it, too. Just point a camera his way and watch the boy pose. He made himself right at home with Dan and Janice's good friends, Mike and Pam Elliott. The Elliotts raised two CCI puppies, one a graduate dog and the other, Milo, released like Romer. Milo and Romer have become good buddies and are certified therapy dogs at Scripps Hospital in Encinitas.

The Flynns got a recent report card on Romer that made them smile like proud parents. Pam wrote:

Romer and I did therapy at Scripps yesterday (Sunday) and he was wonderful. Such a big hit. In one of the rooms he lay down on the extra bed, and the patient rolled him over and rubbed his belly. I know you can picture the way he looked, his paws bent over in the cute, relaxed pose they always do. She fell absolutely in love with him. It was one of our best visits. We're starting to get the hang of this now. I always think of you when I'm doing therapy with him. He's such a joy to be with, and I thank you all the time for the gift of such an awesome addition to our family.

❤

The jury is still out on Flynn dog number ten, a female golden retriever who answers to "Raive." Janice gives her a 50-50 chance of graduating. But Dan is more optimistic, pointing out that she is the most secure puppy they've ever had. "Our granddaughter, Samantha, tipped over a small baby stroller onto Raive, but she didn't even move when it fell on her," Dan says. But Raive was used to Samantha; the two were babies together. In the year that followed, Raive tolerated being crawled over, sat on, pulled, and even being used as a pillow when Sam watched TV. "Samantha learned to throw balls and toys; Raive learned to fetch. They were great together."

Their newest puppy-in-training is Kellin, a male Labrador/golden retriever cross. "He seems very calm at nine weeks of age, loves to be held, and already sleeps through the night," says Dan. "We're still in our first week with him and the bonding process has begun as well as lessons, including recognizing his name; toileting on command; no mouthing, growling, or barking during play; and accepting his leash."

Dan knows that you can't make any predictions in the first week, but says Kellin is off to a great start. He's even heading for the patio door when it's time to potty. Better yet, he hasn't had even one accident in the house.

Good dog.

A Salute to CCI

As for the reason I devoted so many strips to CCI . . . it was my way of honoring Charles and Jeannie Schulz. I met Charles "Sparky" Schulz in 1985, the year Luann began, and over the decades we became friends. I visited the CCI campus in Santa Rosa several times—in fact, that's the last place I saw Sparky, just weeks before his passing. After his death, I wanted to do something that would have made him smile, so I came up with the story line about Luann's friend, Bernice, raising a CCI puppy. I got a huge response from this series—not only from CCI itself, but also from puppy raisers and the lucky few who are the recipients of these fabulous dogs. I like to think Sparky would have called and said, "Good grief! Thanks for the plug!"

LOVE HEELS · Tales from Canine Companions for Independence

Release Dogs

He was smart, good natured, and loved being with humans, loved that better than playing with other dogs.

Release Dogs Not every puppy has the right temperament, talent, or physical qualifications for placement through CCI programs. Puppies that don't graduate are returned to the families or individuals who raised them.

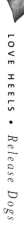
Until We Meet Again

Josh was fun to cuddle, fun to talk to, and, if you believed the book that came with this huge, stuffed dog, everything was going to be all right. But Josh wasn't real and everything wasn't going to be all right. Not in the end.

On the long and painful journey that lay ahead, a real dog named Apache would adopt three-year-old Grant Reed-Plouffe and the rest of his family. Apache made a lot of things all right.

In the months that unfolded, through all the painful hospital procedures and all the sleepless nights, the dog and the boy were inseparable. The only thing Apache couldn't do was to make Grant's pain go away. Ease it, yes. There were moments when the frail boy wrapped his body around the dog, seeking comfort. Everything, the boy whispered to the dog, was going to be all right because he loved Apache "to the moon and back." He always ended his nightly conversations to Apache with that promise, the same exact words from a favorite storybook about a boy and his grandfather.

"A faithful friend is the medicine of life." —Apocrypha

Apache, a CCI release dog, was loved to the moon and back. In return, the Labrador mix hardly ever left the boy's side. They were a team, Superman and his sidekick. Apache was a Lois Lane of Labs, just plain Labradorable.

Apache started life as a Canine Companion for Independence puppy-in-training. He was smart, good natured, and loved being with humans, loved that better than playing with other dogs, Sue Moore remembers. Moore and Creighton Helsley have raised ten puppies for the CCI program, and they agree to this day that Apache remains the smartest dog and the one with the most promise. But his hips, when tested, were not strong enough to pull a wheelchair, and ruined his chances of

More than anything, he told his mom, he wanted a *real* dog.

becoming a Canine Companion. He was released from the program.

The puppy raisers were devastated when they got the call that Apache would be coming home. But in their hearts, the two wanted to bring him home. It had been tough to hand over their canine kid just the month before.

But there was another side. A voice inside Moore's head reminded her that this was a soul that had come into this world with a job to do, and she was pretty sure that job wasn't to be her pet. Someone needed Apache, she told Southwest Regional Center puppy program manager Jeanie Clark. And, just as important, Apache needed to work.

The same time Moore received her call, Grant's parents were faced with more bad news from doctors at Children's Hospital in San Diego. Their young son had a brain tumor that seemed determined to claim him. The disease ravaged the boy's body, leaving him limp. But his spirit refused to give up or give in.

Grant lay on the couch, hugging Josh, just as he

always had in the early stages of his disease, before it was diagnosed. The youngster was only three years and nine months old when the brain tumor was discovered. During his many hospital stays, the boy had always perked up when a therapy dog came to visit. The change in the boy was nothing short of miraculous, and that change was not lost on his mother.

Grant called his mother over to his side one day and whispered a secret wish. His voice was quiet, lest he offend the stuffed friend that had been with him since the first of the pain. More than anything, he told his mom, he wanted a *real* dog.

Those words sent his mother on a mission. She was going to find Grant a dog of his very own, but where? She went searching for a gentle dog that would understand her son's fragile body and equally strong spirit. A friend at the hospital told her about an organization called Canine Companions for Independence. She called to find out about getting a dog for Grant. But he didn't need a helper, he needed a companion. It would be the first time she would tell anyone that her son had cancer, the first time she said the words out loud.

Grant's mother was told that the waiting list for a dog was three years. She heard herself saying that she didn't know if her son had that long.

But what about the dogs who don't make the cut, the ones that flunk out? A lot of people call asking that same question. The organization calls them release dogs. Rarely are these puppies in need of a home. Puppy raisers are given the first right of refusal if their dogs are released from the program. And, as most puppy raisers will tell you, the dogs are like their children. If they can't keep them, they give them to a parent or sibling. These amazing dogs tend to stay in the family.

But, armed only with the determination of a mom's desire to make a son's wish come true, Darla Reed-Plouffe listened to the odds and continued to make her pitch. CCI graduate coordinator Tamara Fleck listened and found herself caught up in the challenge of finding Grant a dog. Apache immediately came to mind, but she said nothing. Fleck took

Fine, the two told Clark later that week, make the telephone call and interview the family. If she and trainer Mary Kay Schneider felt it was a good match, give Apache to Grant.

The couple received an evaluation the next day. They were told it was an incredible family and that Apache was both wanted and needed.

On later visits to the Reed home, the seasoned puppy raisers were sure they had made the right decision. Apache knew from the minute he saw Grant that the boy needed him, Moore says. The two families kept in touch by e-mail and telephone. It was a perfect match.

Other than going home at night, Apache was always in the hospital with Grant. Grant and Apache, aka Superman and his sidekick, were summoned over the hospital's loudspeaker when they were needed in the lab or playroom. In the beginning, Grant wore his Superman T-shirt. Later, it was replaced by a fancy costume with bulging muscles. Ditto for Apache. One of the lab technicians, Daryl, would bend the needle after removing it from Grant's arm and rib the boy of steel for bending

Grant and Apache, aka Superman and his sidekick, were summoned over the hospital's loudspeaker when they were needed in the lab or playroom.

the problem to puppy program manager Jeanie Clark. She, in turn, called Moore and Helsley and told them about the call from Grant's mother. They listened but didn't say much; both needed to think it over. Helsley agonized, debating about what was best for Apache. Moore was sure that Apache had found his calling as a buddy and helpmate for a young boy named Grant.

yet another needle. Grant would giggle, and his mother would laugh.

But giggles and laughs became fewer and farther between as the tumor claimed more and more of Grant's brain. In January 2000, Grant was admitted into the hospital with a blood infection.

One evening Guy and Darla Reed-Plouffe brought Apache to the hospital to visit their son. Apache jumped up on Grant's bed just as the oncologist walked into the room. The doctor smiled, turned away, and gave the two of them time to cuddle before examining Grant.

It was easy to see that when Grant was feeling bad, Apache was the best medicine. When Grant napped, Apache napped, placing his paw on the boy's chest. Grant would smile and tell his parents that Apache was hugging him. And then he would whisper to the dog

ried it in his mouth and wandered through the house. We were all grieving in our own way, Grant's mom says.

At Grant's service, family and friends gathered at the train station in Old Poway Park. Grant had called the steam engine the Thomas Train and loved going round and round the park seated next to the engineer. At the end of the service, the train made one more loop around the park to drop Grant off in heaven. This day, Apache took Grant's place seated next to the engineer.

It was easy to see that when Grant was feeling bad, Apache was the best medicine. When Grant napped, Apache napped, placing his paw on the boy's chest.

that he loved him "all the way to the moon and back."

Apache understood that Grant couldn't play like other kids, couldn't run, couldn't hop, and couldn't play hide-and-seek. But the two were content to watch TV, arms and paws wrapped around one another. And Apache lay right by Grant while he played with his trains. Grant loved his trains; always had since he was a toddler.

Grant was diagnosed with a brain tumor in June of 1999. He and Apache became best friends two months later. Grant died on May 31, 2001.

The day after Grant died, a change came over Apache. He searched the house for Grant, settling for one of the boy's favorite beanie baby toys. He car-

Grant's gravesite reads simply, "Until we meet again." Grant and Apache—Superman and his sidekick—are pictured together in costume.

Although he was Grant's dog, Apache has done a lot for the rest of the family, according to his mother. During those two-plus years of ups and downs, she remembers lots of times when she was afraid. She allowed herself to cry when she held the dog, drying her tears and putting on a reassuring face for Grant. Apache is still offering his own special brand of comfort. She cuddles him daily and thanks him for giving her son so much joy during the last years of his young life.

The Peaceful Warrior

The nose knows. Long before the four-legged thief spotted the food, the aroma of lamb-and-rice kibble wafted though the forest until it found its target. Perfect pouches of breakfast, lunch, and dinner, enough for two days, were there for the chomping in one gluttonous feast.

And so she did. The ravenous raccoon had left the cupboard bare. No food for Hana, a Labrador/golden retriever mix who has been known to inhale her food quicker than any vacuum on the market, then look up as if she hadn't been fed for days. Pitiful.

Jim Gahen, a lifestyle strategist and cofounder of the International Coaching Society, had brought Hana on a New Warrior training adventure, a weekend in the mountains sponsored by the Mankind Project. The program offers men the opportunity to look at their lives, see what's working and what's not, and then map out changes. Jim is on staff; Hana was there on vacation, the only invited female within miles.

"Who is the happy Warrior? Who is he that every man in arms should wish to be?"—William Wordsworth

Hana had come into Jim's life only a few weeks before, a CCI release dog with more medical problems that the program allowed. Colorado puppy raisers Dave and Sue Calvano were put in touch with Jim and Kathy Gahen through a friend. The California couple was searching for a dog to train for therapy work, and it seemed to be a perfect match.

A weekend separation seemed an eternity because the twosome of Jim and Hana had just begun to bond. Jim asked the leader if he could bring Hana, insisting she wouldn't be any trouble. Sure, came the reply, bring her along. The seven-month-old black Lab mix was as welcome as Santa Claus in December.

Jim packed Hana's blanket, a few toys, and a plastic pouch filled with food, and off they drove to the isolated campground. One staff member drove up in a roomy RV and offered Hana a spot to snooze on the cozy couch while the men conducted business. If this was camping, Hana was in heaven.

Then it all came crashing down around dinnertime. That's when Jim discovered the cupboard was bare. Somebody spotted the raccoon and chased it from camp. But the damage had been done. The unrepentant thief would have been chewing on an after-dinner mint if one had been provided.

It looked bad for Hana, but this story is about blessings in disguise. Hana wiggled and wormed her way into the hearts of five dozen men that day. It's well known that the way to a man's heart is through his stomach. And Hana's empty stomach was speaking their language.

Jim salvaged a handful of doggie treats and filled her empty bowl with carrot bits and apple bites. Rabbit food. Hana's weekend menu had turned vegetarian.

Baloney, spelled b-o-l-o-g-n-a.

Hana parked her body under the buffet table and focused on plates filled to overflowing with meats, cheese, breads, and chips. Her tail wagged an SOS beat every time a weekend warrior glanced into her pleading eyes. But the men ignored her; they were under strict orders not to hand-feed the dog table scraps. She would be fed later.

And the "no feed" orders worked, until one man's foot edged too far to the left, placing Hana's tail between a leather sole and a hard rock. The puppy let out a wail, then another even more piercing than the first. Conversation stopped. The men rushed to her aid like so many protective fathers. Hana whim-

pered, and a hand from the guilty party slipped her a piece of yummy bologna. She whimpered again— more meat. This was no dumb dog.

Hana turned pure ham. She weaved through the crowd, never begging, not exactly. She was just there in case anyone wanted to contribute to her well-being. By the end of dinner, Hana had become one of the boys.

The next morning, the men returned to their work, and Hana parked her full tummy on the comfy couch and set her inner alarm clock for lunch. The group was in the middle of an exercise when one of the elders, a retired military colonel, instructed Jim to go get Hana. Colonel Jack barked the order as only a seasoned warrior can. Jim got Hana.

Silently, Hana made her way to the colonel and sat at his side. Colonel Jack led Hana to a middle-aged man with his back to them. Hana stopped and sat. The colonel instructed the man to turn around and open his eyes, saying he had someone he wanted him to meet.

The circle of men were startled as the man whirled around and dropped to his knees. He wrapped his arms around the puppy as if she were a life preserver. The sight of Hana yanked the man back a lifetime ago; back to when he was a kid with a furry pal named Charlie. He had told all his secrets to Charlie, all his fears and silly dreams, and he remembered never once feeling judged. It had been ages, the man confessed, ages since anyone or anything had touched his soul.

Jim felt his eyes fill with tears as he glanced around the circle of men. Amazing, he thought to himself, almost everyone had the same reaction. And that was the day that Hana truly became one of the warriors, a young guide who had the key to the door all of them had come to pass through. Safe passage with Hana, the word got around. Men began to request

Her special talent is in helping these men go back to a simpler time when the love for a first dog was pure happiness.

the weekend when Hana would be part of the staff.

Yep, staff. Hana is the first and only female staff member to go through the weekend initiation process. Her special talent is in helping these men go back to a simpler time when the love for a first dog was pure happiness. It opens their hearts, allowing them to take a good, hard look at where their lives have taken them. Miracles happen during these weekend retreats, even to the colonel. Whenever he speaks Hana's name, the lines in his face relax from "attention" to "at ease."

As for Jim, Hana has worked her magic on him, too. His first black Lab was a dog named Sierra. It's been five long years between dogs, but Jim says he wasn't ready to love again before Hana. Hana is like an updated version of Sierra with all the bells and whistles of next-generation technology, he laughs. She was well trained by the Calvano family, and Jim continues the regimen. The two families e-mail often, communicating in words and pictures.

But there is more to this paw pal than her easy temperament, her willingness to follow commands, even her unending compassion. She is teacher as well as pupil. The lessons have been well taught and well learned, says Jim. Lessons like "Reward the behavior you want in yourself and others." And, by the same token, "Don't dwell on or reward the behaviors you don't want." That goes for Hana, Jim, and his clients.

In everyday life, everyone's behavior has a specific result or reward in mind, Jim insists. And if you think that's baloney, just ask the ham.

Old Smokey

Smokey came into the world as an old man in a canine costume, much like a favorite grandpa whose outside is wrinkled and worn from so much loving. He snuggled up to his first puppy raiser and settled in, nipping at the heels of the family's maternal German shepherd, Mechen, who happened to be another old soul.

But Mechen's bones were old and her muscles were achy. She couldn't tolerate the puppy's adolescent antics and endless energy when her arthritis flared. And so, at the ripe age of nine months (the "troubled teens" in people years), Smokey had worn out his welcome. The tough decision was made to find this Canine Companion a new puppy raiser.

It was a tearful choice for Adrienne Dibsie and her young son, Cole. At age seven, Cole had to learn that he couldn't always do what he wanted. Sometimes, doing the right thing means putting the other guy first, and it hurts. Mechen, they agreed, came first.

"Until one has loved an animal, a part of one's soul remains unawakened." —Anatole France

The young pup had a lot of fans and a long list of potential parents. In class, on puppy outings, and at play group, the little black Lab had earned a reputation for his wise and wayward ways. The pup had spunk and all the right stuff to eventually wear a blue CCI graduate cape.

LeAnn and Kevin Buchanan were selected to finish training the dog. Smokey would be LeAnn's second CCI pup. Hyatt, her first CCI trainee, was a mischievous male, willful and full of wonder, much like Smokey. They had recently turned him

Arlene Kelso, LeAnn Buchanan's grand-mother, is one of Smokey's biggest fans. He is a regular visitor at her assist-ed living center.

Smokey's no fool; a few cookies will buy his undivided attention. But his unconditional love is free for the wanting.

back over to CCI for advanced training. It was LeAnn, loving and brisk but no-nonsense, who made the little Lab toe the line.

And then there was Kevin the mailman, the apple of Smokey's eye. This human playmate was different. He didn't bark orders or make him mind, and best of all, Kevin never turned down a game of fetch. The guy adored Smokey, and Smokey made all the right moves to wrap the unsuspecting mailman around his little paw. Pathetic to watch and hopeless to change, Kevin's wife said.

The loving was lavish and the living was good; the little Lab grew into adulthood. He learned his lessons

well, and the Buchanans shed a lot of tears the day they turned him in for advanced training. This was one dog they just knew wouldn't be released and returned home to them.

But Smokey did come home, less than a month after he was turned in. His x-rays showed that his hips were not strong enough to meet CCI's rigid standards. Service work, which sometimes means pulling a wheel-chair, would have harmed Smokey's health, and so he was released.

And home where he belongs, LeAnn is quick to add. She knew he was more than just a pet. Something about his demeanor told her to find some work for the boy. The idea jelled on a trip to the assisted living center to which her ninety-year-old grandmother, Arlene Kelso, had recently moved. Arlene loved to pet the dog, took him for walks, and never stopped gabbing to the other residents about her granddaughter and the amazing dog she had trained.

The three would cruise the halls looking for people who wanted a visit from Smokey. Lots of people did. LeAnn watched the change that came over their faces when they saw the dog. She noticed that lots of people had lots of names for her boy, most of them the names of dogs they had once loved and lost.

She has given up correcting them and lets the dog be whoever they need him to be during the visit. Occasionally, someone will lead the dog to a chair and carry on a private conversation. She has no idea what they're telling Smokey and he's not talking, which is probably why they confide in him anyway.

Smokey has his favorites, like the lady down the hall from his grandmother. If she doesn't come looking for Smokey, Smokey goes looking for her. Then one day LeAnn spotted her taking a stash of dog biscuits from her dresser drawer. Smokey's no fool; a few cookies will buy his undivided attention. But his unconditional love is free for the wanting.

LeAnn was shocked, not by Smokey's behavior but by her own. She found that she loved watching Smokey visit, especially when he was with people who seemed alone and forgotten. She came away feeling good all over and decided to enroll Smokey as a therapy candidate at a number of local hospitals. Some hospital staffs make dogs pass difficult and advanced training tests; others just want a friendly pet with a health certificate.

No matter where Smokey tested, the bright Lab made sport of the tests and scored nearly perfect marks. None of that surprised LeAnn. If not for his marginal hips, Smokey would have been tops in his CCI graduating class.

Smokey is a working dog doing what he was born to do—helping emotionally and physically ailing people with his winning ways. Even the staff takes time out to fill up on puppy love. Most people tear up when they see Smokey in the hospital. The tears aren't necessarily sad; it's just that this dog strikes a chord so near everyone's heart and soul.

For a brief moment, Smokey can even make a dying man remember the sweetness of life. There was such a man. He couldn't talk, but his wife asked if the dog could come up onto the bed. Smokey obliged, ever so gently, and the wife held her husband's hand and stroked the dog's soft coat. The man smiled, and his wife thanked Smokey for giving her husband a moment of joy.

Smokey is the best definition of pure love there is, according to LeAnn. And she has changed, too, since she and Smokey became a team. Her friends describe her as being more trusting, open, and vulnerable, virtues she once dismissed as too soft.

Perhaps it's the wisdom that comes with age. Nah, it's Smokey.

smokey

LOVE HEELS • Tales from Canine Companions for Independence

Facility Teams

Gentle. Mellow. Those pleading eyes persuaded people to stretch and work through the pain.

Facility Team In this type of team, adults who work as rehabilitation professionals, caregivers, or educators join forces with Canine Companions to improve the mental, physical, or emotional health of those in their care.

Season's Greetings

ebin

The kennel staff lovingly called him Pigpen during the months between "turn in," the beginning of advanced training, and graduation. Ebin knew his way around a mud puddle but never seemed to make it past one without stirring the water from the tip of his pink nose to the end of his blonde tail. Fact was, the only thing more tempting than a puddle of water was a slop of soupy mud. That's where the staff would find Ebin, nine times out of ten.

Even when he was combed and dry, his hair stuck out all over, just begging for someone to stroke it. And, in Ebin's case, the more somebody's stroking his wiry hair the better he likes it. Now he gets strokes from a whole classroom of children. Happy as a pig in mud, Ebin is. So are his kids.

"God gave you a gift of 86,400 seconds today. Have you used one to say thank you?"—William Ward

Ebin passed months of teaching and testing, earning his blue cape last year as a facility dog. With his CCI graduate cape comes a lifetime of love and responsibility. Teacher Janine Shelton and Ebin spend their days in the special education classroom at a middle school in northern California.

Last December, Shelton jotted down some thoughts on the difference Ebin has made in the lives of her special children and put them on a holiday card. The card was a "very big" thank you to friends and CCI family. It was signed:

To: Ebin

From Franco,
who needs Ebin to give him the confidence to be out in wide-open spaces.

From Sarah,
who now lets Ebin lean into her without being afraid, and even calls him over to her desk to sit with her.

From Victor,
whose laughter is infectious when Ebin is nearby.

From Jonathan,
who just started saying the word "doggie."

From Chris,
who speaks louder when he's giving commands to Ebin.

From Stephanie,
who used to need Ebin to quiet her down when she was upset. She doesn't cry at school anymore. No need, now that Ebin's there.

From Esteban,
who believes Ebin has picked him as his favorite because "Ebin always comes to me for a head massage."

From Alexander,
who takes Ebin to doctor's appointments to ease his fears.

From John,
who works hard to speak clearly so Ebin can understand him.

From Zachery,
who is willing to work a little bit harder if it means playing with Ebin when he's finished.

And from the staff, Janine, Melissa, and Keri
who find a calm and happy retreat whenever Ebin is within arm's reach.

romer
The Golden Touch

Barbara Richman held her beloved Romer close to her heart as the Labrador retriever closed his eyes for the last time. She brushed the tears from her cheek and talked about the past few months working alongside the Lab with the golden touch.

She remembers kissing Romer goodbye after their unhurried farewells. She remembers putting his collar, leash, and blankets away. But most of all, Richman remembers the emptiness. Even now, a year later, the tears come before the smiles. But the smiles turn into grins when she talks about the dog with the amazing spirit. In the last months of his life, Romer did the work he was born, bred, and brought up to love.

Romer's first job teamed him with a disabled partner, but that came to an end after six years. He was returned to Canine Companions for Independence. There, Romer was retrained as a facility dog.

"Peace is not found in what surrounds us, but in what we hold within." —Anonymous

About the same time, Richman applied to work with a graduate dog. The five-time puppy raiser wanted to be part of a graduate team helping people recover from injuries or illnesses at Scripps Hospital in Encinitas, California. When Richman saw Romer, she knew she'd met her match. Perfect size, perfect temperament. Perfect partner. The pair graduated after two weeks of intense training at CCI's Oceanside regional facility in November 1998.

Because of his early working years, Romer was at ease around noisy medical equipment and moving wheelchairs. On command, he would gently leap up onto a hospital bed and remain still while a patient stroked his body.

Romer was a favorite with cancer patients, even before they learned that he suffered from the same disease. His first symptoms were subtle—labored breathing and lethargy. Richman expected that it was something simple, something ordinary and easily treatable. But that wasn't the news she was given.

Romer was ill. Terminal—maybe two months, not more, the veterinarian told her. The cancer had inched its way around his lungs and was closing in at a fast pace. It was too late for chemotherapy. Richman

One of the cancer patients he visited at Scripps was Annie Cole. "The closest I came to an animal since I was hospitalized was the cat hair on my quilt," says Cole, who lost her hair to chemotherapy. She whisked her blonde wig from her bald head and plopped it on Romer during their last visit. Romer never moved in protest. "Romer was a great motivator, helping patients focus on him during therapy instead of their own pain," Richman says.

Gentle. Mellow. Those pleading eyes persuaded people to stretch and work through the pain, according to physical therapist Rebecca Pratt. She watched

She watched Romer work his magic on people who had given up on life. He helped some patients walk and others talk after strokes or brain injuries.

walked out of the vet's office, determined to give back to Romer all that he had given to others. He was going to finish his days living a life of leisure.

The next few days she tried pampering the pooch, but Romer had other ideas. "He didn't want to be pampered, he wanted to keep doing what he'd always done," Richman says. "Mornings, he would run for his leash and wait by the door. I decided to keep doing whatever he wanted in the time we had left together." They kept working until the disease brought Romer more pain than pleasure. And then she held his trusting body gently as the veterinarian set his soul free.

The last months were precious. The two walked slower, and Richman parked closer to the hospital door. Romer's ball and tug toys were retired. But there was nothing retiring about Romer. "If anything, Romer breathed easier after he made his rounds," Richman says.

Romer work his magic on people who had given up on life. He helped some patients walk and others talk after strokes or brain injuries. One stroke patient, who insisted he couldn't move an arm, reached out to pet Romer as he wandered by. The desire to touch the dog was stronger than his belief that he couldn't move.

Richman grins when telling the story about an elderly man who hadn't spoken a complete sentence in the months she had been volunteering at the hospital. He sat mute, eyes glazed, as a therapist worked with color cards to jog his memory. On a particularly sunny day, Romer wandered into view, and the old man's eyes locked onto the dog. The man began an animated conversation with the dog as if the two had been old friends.

Richman confesses that the incident caught her off guard and frightened her at first. Then she chalked it off to just another one of "Romer's little miracles." The man didn't stop chatting for a long

romer

Pena
1·03

while, Richman laughs. "And that's Romer's legacy. If dogs could be saints, Romer would be a saint."

In time, Romer's eyes told Richman it was time to say his goodbyes. She took him to see his former CCI graduate teammate, Melanie Watson. The young woman was born with a genetic bone disease that kept her from growing taller than three feet. Her bones break easily, and it was because of her fragile physical condition that the two parted after six years together. "Sometimes, when I was really having a bad life, Romer and I would put my wheelchair in the car and

we'd just go somewhere, even camping," Watson says. One of their proudest moments came in the summer of 1996 when the two carried the Olympic torch a mile through the streets of Los Angeles.

In honor of Romer, Richman helped create a commemorative park at CCI's Oceanside campus. A courtyard salutes years of love and lives watched over with messages engraved in terra-cotta. The gift that Romer gave her is hope, Richman says, "hope that we all can be better than we think we can."

Skilled Companion Teams

"My dog is always happy and he helps me to get stuff. It used to be harder for me when I dropped something or wanted to open a door."

Skilled Companion Team This team has three members: a child or an adult with physical, developmental, or emotional disabilities; a primary caretaker; and a Canine Companion who helps with physical tasks and creates a bond of companionship, affection, and love.

Matt's Odyssey

Cheating death? Yes, Matt Thompson has done it twice; three times if you count the day his heart stopped at the thought of losing the big, black Lab that he had come to think of as his own.

The dog wasn't his, not really. Not yet, anyway. He and his mom had spent the first of two weeks at team training, a rigorous course that partners Canine Companions with people with disabilities.

The teenager was born with spina bifida and scoliosis. He is paralyzed from the waist down, has poor eyesight, and a life-threatening allergy to latex. But his heavy burden of physical challenges, seventeen surgeries, and twenty-two hospitalizations was a mere blip on the screen compared with the probability of losing his Lab, Odyssey. Just Ody, for short.

"Don't be afraid to take a big step if one is indicated. You can't cross a chasm in two small steps." —David Lloyd George

Matt buried his face in Ody's black fur and wept. In less than forty-eight hours, he would have to say goodbye to the dog. Matt was inconsolable. The Lab put his head on the boy's lap and snuggled, careful not to injure the boy's frail legs.

How had it happened? How could something that seemed so right go so wrong?

Norie Thompson had left CCI Southwest Regional Center in Oceanside, California, in the late afternoon. Matt was buckled into his seatbelt; Ody had her body curled around the boy's feet. The plan was to spend the night at home to let Matt and Ody bond and practice working as a team. Everyone in the class was allowed to take his or her companion home overnight, then report back the next morning with questions and doubts.

Norie phoned home to tell her husband, Rick, and younger son, Ethan, that they were on their way. She wanted the homecoming to be smooth and safe and had left strict instructions.

The two-hour ride to the family's home was uneventful. Every now and then, the mother glanced into the van's rearview mirror, warmed by the contentment on her son's face. He had been sure there was a black Lab just right for him and told her so the week before on the sixty-mile drive to the training facility. His eyes lit up the first time he spotted Odyssey in a kennel, and he hadn't taken his eyes off her the whole week.

Her eyes, mind, and feet were racing in different directions. In all the commotion, she tripped and fell. Norie remembers trying to soften the inevitable collision with the cement sidewalk by using her arms as cushions. She landed hard, but her body was pumping out so much adrenaline that she felt fine. Surprised, she got up and brushed herself off.

She opened the back of the van to get Matt's wheelchair, scooped her son up in her arms, and settled him in his chair. Then she gave Ody the command to get out of the van and heel. After she got everyone settled, she swallowed a couple of aspirins and napped on the couch.

Two hours later, Norie knew she was in trouble.

It was clear that Ody belonged with Matt; it was that simple. After all their son had been through, Matt needed to love this dog and be loved back unconditionally.

Matt was ecstatic when trainers paired the two just the Wednesday before. Now, they were headed out for their first unsupervised adventure, with no tests to pass and nothing to prove. All was right with the world. They were headed home.

Father and younger son scurried to straighten the house and yard for the homecoming. When the van pulled into the driveway, Rick was mowing the grass and the house was full of Ethan's young playmates. The doors to the house were wide open; the gates to the backyard were both ajar.

Norie says the chaotic sight set her off, causing her to lose her cool. The dog jumped up to find out what all the commotion was about; Matt just rolled his eyes. Norie got out of the van, her frustration mounting. Nothing was going by the book, as she had promised herself. She turned to quiet Odyssey.

Her arms were in spasms so severe that her husband couldn't move her. An ambulance took her to a nearby hospital, where doctors put words to her pain: fractured left wrist and elbow, severely sprained right wrist and elbow, and severe muscle shock in both arms.

Matt was still awake when his mother returned from the hospital at midnight. He was crying; he had never seen his mom hurt. She was the one who was always there to offer comfort and to promise that everything would be all right. But this time, she had to tell him that it wasn't going to be all right; they would have to drop out of team training. Odyssey would have to go back and finish the training with someone else.

The next day, the trainers agreed it was best to wait six months or so to allow Norie's body to heal before returning to try again. They offered to let

Odyssey go home with Matt as long as they brought her back on Monday.

Matt was utterly devastated and turned to Ody for comfort. He had already waited three years for a dog, and the thought of waiting another six months was too much to bear. The dog knew something was wrong and sat very still on the bed next to Matt. Norie says Ody knew her son was hurting; the dog offered him the comfort he so desperately needed.

On Sunday, Rick and Norie knew that their son couldn't and wouldn't lose that dog—not if they could do anything about it. It was clear that Ody belonged with Matt; it was that simple. After all their son had

been through, Matt needed to love this dog and be loved back unconditionally. The way Norie saw it, her son was now a teenager and, like all adolescents, he was exercising his independence. He needed someone like Ody to help him deal with pain and loneliness that most kids couldn't even imagine.

Rick phoned his office and arranged for an emergency vacation. The next day, all three of them drove up to complete the last week of team training. When they arrived, staff volunteers gathered to say their goodbyes. Classmates presented Matt with a stuffed black Lab puppy; the trainers had already packed their supplies.

But the Thompsons had other ideas, and they told the trainers their new plan. It didn't go over well; the trainers didn't see how Norie could continue with both arms injured. Norie had removed the soft cast from her right arm and told them her left hand wasn't as bad as it looked; it didn't really hurt. Inside her head, a voice whispered that most of it was true, her pain was nothing compared with all the hurt her son had endured. She forced a smile and wouldn't take no for an answer. The trainers relented and offered to give it a try.

The necessary leash corrections pulled on Norie's muscles and sent them into spasms. The only relief from the pain was her son's knowing smile. Norie says that every time she looked at her son's face, she knew they had made the right decision. She had been at Matt's side when his pain had seemed too much to bear; now, he told her, it was his turn to be the strong one. She never pretended the pain wasn't there, and, with the tables turned, their bond deepened. Matt brushed her arm with his hand as she had done for him so many times before when his pain seemed endless. He knew just how big the sacrifice was; he understood her pain.

Monday lasted an eternity; Tuesday wasn't any easier. By Wednesday, Norie had settled into a painful groove; the time came and went. Thursday's tests were a challenge, but the family passed. Friday was one day before graduation. Having come so far, Norie says, she could have endured any amount of pain.

Their graduation ceremony in May 2001 was memorable. When Odyssey's leash was officially turned over to Matt, the Lab nuzzled her nose in his lap, looked up, and licked his face. The audience stood and gave the team a raucous ovation.

The family had accomplished the seemingly impossible. Matt was their role model; he had spent a lifetime conquering the seemingly impossible and so he led the way. Matt and Ody were the teachers; Mom and Dad the proud pupils who learned firsthand that sometimes you have to risk taking a giant step when little steps just won't get the job done.

Matt almost died twice on the operating table but lived to tell about it. He doesn't talk a lot about that or what other people label "disabilities." Getting around in a wheelchair seems normal to him; everyone else is just "temporarily able bodied" (TABs for short).

Matt likes what other kids like—computer games, surfing the Net, and playing soccer, basketball, and tennis. The only difference is he does these sports sitting down. Odyssey likes any activity where there are lots of children in wheelchairs. She nuzzles her face in their laps so it's easier for them to scratch behind her ears. A wheelchair camp is Ody's idea of heaven, Norie says. And Matt doesn't mind sharing her affection with his brother Ethan and his friends.

The serious Lab and the serious boy are inseparable. Ody has made it possible for Matt to live a more independent life, and for this his parents will always be thankful. Special mention should be made of the great job she does retrieving for Matt. Because he has a metal rod in his spine to correct his scoliosis, it is hard for Matt to bend sideways. Even dropping a pencil used to be a major frustration for him. Now he smiles as Ody picks up whatever he accidentally drops. She can even hand him her food bowl.

Even Norie's accident was a blessing, of sorts. She knows that if she hadn't fallen, Rick wouldn't have participated so fully in the program. Because it brought the family closer together, Norie says she's glad it happened. Turns out that Rick, Norie, Ethan, Matt, and Odyssey make a great team.

Maybe, Maybe Not

Jonathan Crumes had waited half his young lifetime to get the nod from his mother for a Canine Companion. Finally, Diana Klein made a call to Canine Companions for Independence in Oceanside, California. It took a few more years before they got the return call to come on down and train with a canine partner.

Klein wanted a special friend for her son, someone to help him with his busy life. No shy dog for this not-so-shy young man, his mom said to instructors at the start of team training in the summer of 2001. Jon, then a seventh grader, required a Canine Companion who would rather be on the go than sit at home.

"This is my dog," twelve-year-old Jon repeated to every trainer, shortly after he went window-shopping through the kennels. He picked what he thought would be the perfect skilled companion dog, telling anyone who would listen that he had found his perfect partner. "That's my dog there," he insisted. The one, he said, that looked the rowdiest.

"There are no mistakes, no coincidences. All events are blessings given to us to learn from." —Elisabeth Kubler-Ross

One of the seasoned trainers smiled at the insistent boy, saying, "Maybe, maybe not." Jon took a spin up and down the training room with a huge golden/Lab cross at the end of the leash. Next, trainers paired him with a smaller black Lab that gracefully put her paws on his lap on command. Finally, he put his electric chair into high gear and took a blonde Lab for a spin around the room.

Did he get a chance to work out with the dog of his dreams?

Maybe, maybe not.

Norway's puppy raisers, Zoe Cryns and her
daughter Miranda, say it was a happy day
when they put their puppy's leash
and life into Jon's hands.

The day passed, then another. More dogs, more potential partners. On the third day, it was time for Jon and the others to write down their top three choices. And so he did. And just to leave no doubt in the trainers' minds, he wrote the same name three times in a row.

Later that night, the trainers gathered to make preliminary matches. A huge drawing board listed the dogs' names on the left and the students on the right, instructor Rhonda Faul says. "Jonathan needed a dog that could help him at home now as well as help him become more independent in the future," she says. "He needed a companion dog to assist him with lots of different tasks."

And, most important, as with all skilled companion placements, Jon needed an assistance dog that responded well to both him and his mother, Diana. She's the one who would set the foundation for the whole working relationship. "Ultimately, the success of this team would depend on Jon and Diana's compatibility with the dog," Faul says.

Did Diana and her son see eye to eye?

Maybe, maybe not.

Jon is quick to tell you that he did get the perfect pooch. But he won't say if Norway was his first choice. It doesn't matter now. Two years have come and gone and Jon says he can't imagine life without Norway.

"I love Norway. We're good together because he helps me to be more independent," Jon says. "My dog

is always happy and he helps me to get stuff. It used to be harder for me when I dropped something or wanted to open a door."

For now, Norway stays with Diana during the day, while Jonathan is off at school. But next year, when Jon enters high school, things may be different. The teen hopes to pass the necessary tests to qualify as Norway's primary handler. "My friends think it would be cool to have my dog in school. He's real popular," adds the gregarious teen.

Diana keeps Norway busy during the day, but by early afternoon, the dog parks himself near the front door and waits impatiently for Jon. His tail picks up speed when he hears the familiar sounds of the school bus.

The two are inseparable as they catch up on the day's happenings. On command, Norway heads to the refrigerator to get a can of soda. Then, Jon gets his buddy a treat and the two go out for some exercise.

Last winter, Norway packed his bag and went along on the family's ski vacation to Colorado. The two boarded the plane and Norway parked his huge body at Jon's feet. Occasionally, Norway took a stroll down the plane's narrow aisle to stretch his legs. The passengers applauded; the flight attendants treated the dog like royalty. And for good reason, Jon smiles. "My dog has a special purpose."

Jon went skiing nearly every day. Norway stayed near as his partner suited up, then waited on the

sidelines as the teen came racing down the hill toward him. Later, the two would romp in the snow. "Jon laughed so hard when we put on Norway's snow boots," Diana says. "He wasn't sure how to walk in them, so he literally danced around; it was the most hilarious thing you ever saw."

Jon still laughs about it today. He knows how very lucky he is to have Norway, his mom says, adding, "We think Norway feels the same way."

Norway's puppy raisers, Zoe Cryns and her daughter Miranda, say it was a happy day when they put their puppy's leash and life into Jon's hands. 🐾

A Friend Indeed

The O'Connor family had lived in the same home for a long time. Joseph, Linda, and their young daughter, Siobhan, took the same walks down the same streets, always with the same empty outcome.

Joseph Karr O'Connor talks about those lonely outings, when neighbors would nod and quicken their steps as they passed by his family. No one ever spoke. Sometimes they stared, but they never spoke. His already ruddy complexion reddens as he relives those walks; his eyes fill with tears as he strokes his daughter's maple brown hair.

Ten-year-old Siobhan (pronounced Shah-von) smiles at her father. Her saucerlike eyes question his dismay. But her lips will never form a question; she was born without the ability to speak. Siobhan has a very rare disorder called cri du chat (cat's cry) syndrome, so called because infants with this syndrome often have a high-pitched cry. Children with cri du chat have physical abnormalities, language and motor skill difficulties, and varying degrees of mental retardation. Siobhan also has another rare disorder, dystonia, which causes her leg muscles to contract and impairs her walking.

"There is no wilderness like a life without friends . . ." —Baltasar Gracian

Although Siobhan may never speak about those things that affect her so deeply, she understands more and more each day. Her parents have taught her a communication system to help her express herself. The Picture Exchange Communication System (PECS) enables Siobhan to communicate.

Siobhan, who was nearly four by the time she learned to walk, climbs into a jogging stroller for after-dinner outings. A few years ago, the youngster began to reach out to people who clearly didn't want to extend a hand in return. Whether it was from discomfort or from not knowing what to say to a nonverbal, retarded child, it all came down to the same thing. Her parents felt hurt, frustrated, and, yes, sometimes more than just a little angry. Siobhan had lived on the same street for many years, but she had never had the opportunity to attend her neighborhood school. She had been to six different programs and four schools since kindergarten, trying to find a teacher who would implement her communication system, and didn't know a single child or adult on her block.

All that's changed since Siobhan met Gaynor. The Labrador retriever was matched as a skilled companion with the young girl during the February 2002 Canine Companions for Independence training class. Gaynor now accompanies her family on the long strolls, and because of her, these walks have changed drastically. Not surprisingly, nearly every passerby stops to pet and chat with the dog.

Not so fast.

If people want to meet the dog, her father decided, they must first go through Siobhan. The youngster understands that almost everyone wants to pet her dog, and she now has the power to communicate a yes or no, or to request that people "shake hands" with Gaynor by using her communication book. The language alternative was employed because Siobhan's poor fine-motor coordination makes signing impossible.

In PECS, thumb-size pictures communicate nouns and verbs. Siobhan picks out a series of words and places them on a Velcro-lined bookmark. When she's finished putting her thoughts into pictures, she hands the bookmark to those asking permission to pet her dog. Sometimes she asks them to shake the dog's hand; sometimes she wants them to pet her head.

And sometimes the answer is no. It's her call, her parents agree.

The growth in her social and verbal skills has been amazing. A few months ago, the only pronoun in her book was "I," and her sentences were two words long. Nouns in her isolated world included postage-size snapshots of relatives. There was nothing to represent "stranger" because strangers didn't play a part in her world. Since Gaynor came on the scene, Siobhan has added the pronoun "you." The concept of "you" is drawn as a hand with a pointed index finger: I want + you + pet + Gaynor = permission to interact with her dog.

Siobhan's communication skills have blossomed in ways her parents had only dreamed would be possible. She's bold about reaching out to strangers, and, with Gaynor at her side, the two make contact with a lot of people. Motivated to communicate, Siobhan can now make four-word sentences.

Strangers need something in common to start a conversation, explains her father, even if it's just waiting for an elevator. He applauds the role that Gaynor plays in his daughter's life. Every social interaction gets Siobhan and the entire family involved in the life of the community. They no longer feel isolated. Some of the neighbors, in fact, are on a first-name basis, and Grace, the little girl who lives across the street, now comes over to play. Grace, Siobhan, and Gaynor make a great ball team. Siobhan throws, Grace shouts, "Get the ball," and Gaynor obliges. Giggles and squeals fill the backyard, with occasional barks when Gaynor is asked to "speak" on the playhouse phone.

Siobhan's communication book has doubled in size since Gaynor joined the family. The youngster always has the book within arm's reach, and her mother says she delights in giving commands. Having Gaynor has improved Siobhan's physical skills and given her age-appropriate responsibilities. Measuring Gaynor's food, brushing her, and putting on her leash and vest have dramatically improved Siobhan's

fine-motor skills. And since she was fitted with leg braces and began receiving botox injections, she has been able to walk alongside Gaynor using the student leash.

Siobhan's world revolves around Gaynor. It's a world growing by leaps and bounds, thanks to her Canine Companion. On late afternoons, when it's cold and windy outside, the two can be found in the family room watching a video. The little girl sits with her legs stretched out to make room for Gaynor's head on her lap.

Siobhan finally has that wonderful teacher who really wants to help her to communicate. She and her family hope that she can soon start bringing Gaynor to school to further develop life skills and to help her get to know the other children.

Supporting Role

tattinger

Service dog Tatty checks to see that his birthday cake has the right number of candles.

Nothing seemed out of the ordinary the day Mary was born. Gary and Teddi Cole gazed at their little girl's chubby face and felt they had been blessed with an angel. Perfect. She had ten fingers, ten toes, and a smile that reduced her daddy to a puddle whenever he looked at her.

Mary cooed, crawled, and walked right on schedule, according to the baby books. But by her second birthday, she had yet to babble her first word. Something is wrong, her mother worried. She'll talk, but in her own time, her father replied.

"When we accept tough jobs as a challenge to our ability and wade into them with joy and enthusiasm, miracles can happen."—Arland Gilbert

Teddi made an appointment with a developmental pediatrician. She needed to know what she could do to help her daughter grow into a self-confident little girl. Gary felt his wife was overreacting but agreed to the testing to help put her mind at ease. The pediatrician put Mary through a battery of tests and came to a conclusion. The diagnosis was devastating—autism. Teddi left the doctor's office in complete denial. Autism seemed like a lifetime sentence, one that would imprison her daughter in loneliness and suffering.

Autism.

The "how" and "why" weren't as important as the "what." Teddi read every book she could find on autism, logged on to the Internet, and devoured every detail about the condition.

Autism.

The label became important. Teddi knew that if she was going to help her daughter, she needed somewhere to start. She needed to know the enemy and meet it on its own terms. The Coles began a very long journey that continues to this day.

The first thing they decided was that they weren't going to isolate their daughter from the real world. Wherever they went, Mary went along, too. Children with autism flap their arms to get a sense of their bodies, Teddi says. And, because of this startling behavior, many parents feel social pressure to keep their children at home. Not the Coles. Teddi believes it's Mary who counts most. She'll never see the other people again, so what does it matter what they think?

Mary's parents are both actors and live in a world where the impossible becomes the possible if your heart wants it badly enough. And their hearts hurt with wanting to give their daughter a future full of hope. They were determined to get Mary every break she needed to be the very best she could be.

Their first pediatrician painted a bleak picture of Mary's future. His prognosis was completely unacceptable, so they found another pediatrician. The second one was willing to talk about the possibilities instead of dwelling on the probabilities.

They enrolled their daughter in a number of therapy programs near their home. Then Gary Cole accepted a movie role that took the family to North Carolina, a hotbed of research in developmental disabilities. The whole family went to work. Gary made a TV movie, *For My Daughter's Honor*, while Mary and Teddi enrolled in an intensive program for autistic children. The one constant, Teddi says, was that every autistic child she met was different from the next.

Fortunately, Mary loved to be around people. She learned to say "Bye-bye, Daddy," and, to her parents, it seemed to open up a world of possibilities. Her vocabulary slowly expanded, but her attention span was short. By her fourth birthday, however, Teddi and Gary were ecstatic at her progress and were able to outline a course of speech and occupational therapy.

But the biggest breakthrough came one evening when the family attended a holiday party at a friend's home. As soon as Mary walked through the door, she spotted the furry animal on the couch. She ran over, sat next to the little dog, and began to entertain it with sing-along snippets from Christmas carols. Daughter and doggy bonded instantly in a way that Mary's parents had never seen before. They stared at their daughter and instantly came to the same conclusion: Mary needed a dog.

But Mary became too animated; the dog took a nip at her. Rather than being frightened, Mary tried to console the animal. Her parents rescued the dog from Mary and tore her away, promising they would find her a doggy of her own.

But it was clear to Teddi that Mary would need a special dog, one with the temperament and training to partner with a special child like Mary.

Again, Teddi turned to the Internet. She called Canine Companions for Independence and arranged to have an application mailed to her. An interview followed within weeks. Teddi's biggest fear was that the group wouldn't think her daughter needed one of their special dogs. They asked her how she thought a dog could benefit Mary, and Teddi recounted the Christmas story.

Mary, she told them, needed a friend who wouldn't judge her if she didn't say something right. Mary needed someone to sing to, but most of all, she needed a bridge to other children. She needed to broaden her world and let other people, especially kids her own age, inside. Nine months later, Mary and Teddi were enrolled in a two-week training program with a promise of a dog at the end of the line.

When Mary loses the feel of where her body is in space, she commands Tatty to "crash," which is the signal for him to gently put his body weight against hers. The pressure of his body helps her reorient herself. After Mary has come to herself again, Tatty gives her a doggy kiss.

And that's when Mary met Tattinger. There was a change in Mary from the moment she put her hand on Tattinger's furry coat. She became calm and focused. It was remarkable. And the remarkable journey continues.

Teddi, Gary, and Mary often speak to large groups about the miracle in their lives since Tatty came to live with them two years ago. Mary is ten now and still looks like an angel. She speaks in sentences; she understands others and can make herself understood. She can count her ten fingers and ten toes and count on Tatty to be right by her side. And when she loses sense of her body, Tatty does a "crash" command until Mary feels settled and safe again. The huge golden retriever gently lowers himself onto her body and stays perfectly still until Mary regains control of herself. He stays until she says "Off."

Mary's world revolves around Tatty, and the two continue to conquer new territory as a working team. This remarkable relationship has confounded and amazed some professionals who work with autistic children.

Nothing confusing about it to Teddi, though. She sits back in wonder as she watches her daughter become more independent every day. Teddi has become an advocate for other children with autism, hoping that more of them can be teamed with companion dogs to help expand their worlds, too.

tattinger

And Teo Makes Three

Teo Hill Kent was raised by an attorney. As a puppy he spent time in a court-room learning the importance of telling the truth, the whole truth, and nothing but the truth.

Perhaps that explains his inability to sidestep the facts. He gets this certain look, a hangdog look, that's a dead giveaway when he's been up to no good. It doesn't happen often; Teo is, by all standards, a very courteous canine. But put a bag of liver treats within nose range, and this curious creature isn't one to ignore the obvious. He'll swipe them. "He ate them all and brought me the empty bag," says Owen Kent, laughing. "I would never have known. He ate them in another room, but he brought me the evidence and put it in my hand."

"One's self-image is very important because if that's in good shape, then you can do anything, or practically anything."—Sir John Gielgud

Owen, who has both the looks and the wisdom of storybook character Harry Potter, laughs a lot these days. It's been a grand adventure since the fourth grader was teamed with Teo at Canine Companions for Independence. Getting Teo, Owen explains, is the best thing that could have happened.

Owen is an only child who lost his mother, Kate, nearly two years ago. Life has been a little lonely, and Owen has had lots of love to spare. But not anymore, not since Teo came into his life.

Harry Kent stands back and watches his son deep in conversation with Teo, and it brings a tear to his eye. It's nice for his son to have another set of ears to tell his troubles, joys, and laments to. "When I see the closeness between the two, it gives me a peaceful feeling," Harry says. "Owen's life is so much more complete."

Owen races around in an electric wheelchair, unwilling to let his disability get in the way of getting around. He's at an age when growing independence is cherished as a rite of passage. Asking for help, especially for the little things, is unacceptable. "You can't just do your life running other people down because you have a disability," he says. "That's not how I'm going to do my life. Everyone needs someone to help them and I have Teo." Teo has tuned into Owen and is ready to help him at the drop of a pencil.

It was love at first sight, too, for puppy raiser Lynne Hill, the attorney who taught Teo right from wrong, left from right, and all about the ups and downs of life. She takes the bow as his puppy raiser and then offers praise to trainer Todd Young at CCI's Southwest Regional Center in Oceanside, California. "Todd will always have my gratitude," she says. "He really worked with Teo during his months of advanced training and the two had a fabulous relationship. I knew he would find a good match for Teo and he did." Hill also applauds the work of Teo's team during the puppy-training months. She calls them Teo's village people.

It takes a whole village to raise a service dog, according to Hill. Each person offers a different experience that adds up to a well-rounded and secure canine. When the puppy's months with Hill came to a close, Teo's graduation picture was taken with seventeen "village people" and their dogs.

Teo and Owen are truly living the good life. And that makes Lynne and Teo's entire village smile.

Lynn Chavez, who was part of that village, laughs about the day she spent sick at home with Teo at her side. A head cold had left her with sniffles and an aching feeling, so she retired to the couch with blankets and a box of tissues. Every time she sneezed, she reached for a tissue to blow her nose. Teo took note. Again and again, he watched the ritual. "I was using the bathroom when I got a sneeze attack," she says. "Teo came strolling in with the box of tissues in his mouth. From that moment on, I never doubted that Teo would make it all the way."

Teo had a huge cheering section when he left the protective custody of his village and went off to college. Although puppy raisers are not allowed to see or visit their dogs during the next six months of training, Teo had lots of aunts and uncles watching out for him and reporting back to Hill.

And there were monthly reports from his trainer, too. Mostly glowing reports. The angel puppy had not strayed from his training and seemed to be enjoying new challenges. He learned to tug, open and close doors, retrieve, and dozens of other tasks. Todd Young found Teo a very willing student. He mastered everything he would need to know to be teamed with a graduate. And so it was that he met his match in Owen Kent.

Hill was happy for the two and a little sad, too. She knew that Teo was never coming home with her; he had another life waiting for him that didn't include her. That's what you hope for, Hill insists; that's the very best outcome for your dog. Still, the finality of saying goodbye comes with a certain amount of selfish pain. Teo had always been such a special dog—still is, just ask Owen.

His dad did. Harry wanted to know what Teo felt like, and the boy replied with a handful of words that said everything there is to say: "Teo feels like love."

"When I found out Teo was placed with a child, I was thrilled because I knew Teo would get and give the love he needed," Hill says. "And it really seems like that has happened. Plus with Harry and Owen, Teo has the best chance of remaining active and interacting with lots of people, the two things he really enjoys."

Harry Kent is a world-class mountain climber and a professional outdoor-adventure guide who operates Kent Mountain Adventure Center in Estes Park, Colorado. The camp provides outdoor experiences for kids to help bolster their self-esteem and athletic abilities.

Teo spends his days with Harry once Owen is dropped off at school. But every day at three o'clock, Teo can be found waiting on the van's lift for Owen to come into sight. He showers Owen with kisses until the young boy giggles. Then it's off for home and homework. There's play, lots of play with swimming and soccer. Last year, the two were invited onto the field to make the "first kick" at a Denver Rapids professional soccer game.

Lynne's job took her to Colorado, and she used the opportunity to drop in on the Kents. "I was thrilled that Teo hadn't forgotten me," she says. "He became very excited and happy to see me. Owen and Harry were generous enough to let me 'dog-sit' for a day, and Teo showed me the sights in Rocky Mountain National Park. We went on a hike, then had lunch in Estes Park."

The next day, Owen, Teo, and Lynne took a Halloween hayride. Lynne and Owen loved the hay, the rocky roads, even the screaming kids. Teo, Lynne says, sat and endured the experience, his tail wagging only at the end of the ride.

Teo and Owen are truly living the good life. And that makes Lynne and Teo's entire village smile.

Little Joe

Nobody told Joseph Cabral much about what he could or couldn't be, mostly because nobody thought it would make any difference. Born with Down's syndrome, Joseph's mother looked at her baby boy as if he were a cross to bear rather than an angel in her midst.

The pretty blonde envisioned a perfect portrait of her family, the stuff of which Hallmark cards are made. But Betty Cabral was jolted from her happily-ever-after fantasy just seconds after the birth of her second child. You could see it in the doctor's face; the nurse's, too. Something was very wrong with Joseph. The diagnosis was dismal: weak muscles, impaired hearing, and limited mental capacity. And two broken hearts. An operation could fix Joseph's heart problem; time and love would have to heal his mother's.

"Create the highest, grandest vision for your life, because you become what you believe." —Oprah Winfrey

It took two weeks for Betty to force herself to enter the baby's room. The torment was unending. Why had this terrible thing happened to her? And when she got past the "why," she could only ask, "Now what?"

Joseph was two months old when God answered her first question. The tiny baby was vomiting violently. Between bouts, Joseph looked into his mother's eyes, trying to catch her gaze. He was trying to smile at her, she says. It was that moment when it occurred to her that none of this was about her. And if she could have a little faith, God would answer the rest of her doubts. This was her baby; he belonged here and she belonged at his side.

trevor

Thinking back to the first week at team training, Betty says her son was smitten with Trevor the moment the dog walked into the room.

As the years unfolded, the son sometimes took on the role of tutor. There is something about this boy of twelve that belies his worldly inexperience. He can see some things so clearly; other things he cannot comprehend at all.

He knows that almost everything can be fixed with a smile, maybe even a hug. He doesn't know why some of the neighborhood kids think they're too big to play with him now. He knows that when you get mad, you yell and then you smile; he doesn't understand why some people get mad and stay mad. And he has taught a lot of people, mostly by example, that you can be whatever you dream you can be. And if you're going to bother to dream, dream big.

His mother worries that the kids he grew up with are at an age when they're moving on to a place where Joseph isn't ready to follow. Someday, she hopes, Joseph will acquire the maturity and skills for independent living, but that day is a long way off. For now, the other kids are growing up and moving on without Joseph.

That's okay with Joseph; he went out and found himself a new best friend named Trevor. Like Joseph, Trevor doesn't understand about staying mad or holding grudges or wearing the latest designer clothes. He doesn't even care whether or not other kids want to play with him. He likes doing whatever Joseph wants to do, as long as they can do it together.

♥

The idea of a Trevor in the Cabral household started out with two strikes against it—Dad figured a dog would be too much added responsibility, and Mom was afraid of dogs. But it was clear that a Canine Companion could help their young son in ways that they couldn't. A man from church had told them about Canine Companions for Independence in Oceanside, California, and suggested they look into the program.

Betty was determined to get over her fear of dogs if her son could benefit from having a service animal. But her husband balked at the idea. Looking back, Betty says it wasn't so much the frustration of having a dog in the house as it was the fear of letting a dog into his heart. Dogs, he confessed, get old too soon,

Trevor has been good for Joseph. His gentle ways calm the boy when he is afraid and keep him centered when his attention is scattered.

then die and break your heart. Eventually he relented; he now admits that the benefits to his son outweigh any later heartache.

The family filled out an application, qualified, and was put on a list. They waited, some of them more patiently than others. Joseph became even more animated; conversations revolved around the arrival of the newest member of the family. The wait lasted a year and a half.

The two-week team-training class was set for March. Betty's world began to fall apart in the closing days of February after her father was diagnosed with kidney cancer. Surgery was scheduled for the same day team training started. Then there was work; the family's tax business was facing the final crunch before Uncle Sam wanted his due. The family needed her at the business; Joseph needed her at team training.

Betty spent her days with Joseph and after-class hours at the hospital with her mother. Luckily, everything turned out all right in the end: her father's operation was a success, Joseph got Trevor, and their clients met Uncle Sam's deadline.

Thinking back to the first week at team training, Betty says her son was smitten with Trevor the moment the dog walked into the room. Joseph called him Trevor Doggy and went looking for him whenever the two were apart.

Trevor is big and brawny. When they were first introduced, Betty approached him hesitantly, but Joseph ran up to him, wrapped his arms around him, and claimed him for his own. The unconditional love ran both ways, and Betty felt pressure to perform and prove to the trainers that she could handle Trevor.

Betty says she had her eye on another dog in the class who was textbook mellow and just as mindful. But the trainers thought Joseph had just too much boundless energy for the low-key canine. So she sucked in her breath and took Trevor's leash. She was determined to do whatever it took to help her child.

Betty says she knew her son *needed* this dog as desperately as he *wanted* Trevor for his new best friend. Joseph gets left behind a lot when childhood friends run off to parties and sleepovers. And not just Joseph; all children with developmental disabilities go through the same trauma of being abandoned by their peers. Kids with Down's go into deep depression over these losses, Betty says. They begin to realize they're different, and it was very painful to watch it happening to Joseph.

Betty worked overtime to get the dog in line, sure that if she didn't make Trevor obey her, then the trainers wouldn't let him come home with Joseph. Failing Joseph was the worst thing in the world, she says, and she wasn't going to let it happen.

Her son took the leash and bossed the dog around. The dog did as the young boy said, waiting for the obligatory scratch behind the ear. His "good dog" rewards were both verbal and physical. And the dog clearly adored the young boy. During breaks, Joseph got down on the floor with his Trevor Doggy and loved him as every dog should be loved.

Trevor has been good for Joseph. His gentle ways calm the boy when he is afraid and keep him centered when his attention is scattered. Trevor is teaching Joseph about responsibility and maturity.

But those "atta boys" have gotten rowdier; Joseph drops to his knees and gets in the dog's face, rubbing him behind both ears and singing his praises. Trevor is amazingly patient with her son, Betty says, even putting up with the myriad costumes that Joseph dresses him in. When Joseph turns Batman, Trevor wears a cape, too. And they have a whole drawerful of T-shirts to share.

Betty says Joseph is learning a lot about himself just by taking care of Trevor. He's more organized and is getting more comfortable offering his dog the discipline that Joseph so desperately needs in his life. Trevor is teaching Joseph to be more at ease with himself during the adolescent years, when so much changes. Having Trevor even makes it easier for Joseph to accept the inevitable "pulling away" of his adored sister, Alexis. Now that she is a teenager, Alexis is beginning to spend more time with her friends and less with Joseph.

Joseph wants Trevor to be with him all the time; he won't go to the school bus stop without his dog. They go on walks and talk, Trevor always doing the listening and Joseph the talking. And the dog has brought Joseph's old pals back on the scene because everyone wants to be around Trevor.

As for Betty, she's enjoying what a wonderful gift Joseph has been and thanks God every day. To her, Joseph is the essence of unconditional love; simple, uncomplicated love.

Just like Trevor, Joseph smiles.

Jacob's Journey

There isn't a whole lot about being a kid that this kid knows a whole lot about; there just hasn't been time between operations and physical therapy. Ten-year-old Jacob Cooper has osteogenesis imperfecta, a brittle-bone disease that makes his body extremely fragile. It's been that way since the day he was born, in a small, rural Ohio community.

Jacob was rushed by ambulance to a big-city hospital, where doctors hooked up his tiny body to a bank of tubes, wires, and machines. Medical staff came and went, shaking their heads. "I remember the next few days so clearly," says his mom, Lisa. "After a while, doctors told me he probably wouldn't live the weekend. They unhooked him from all the equipment, wrapped him in a blanket, put him in my arms, and said good luck."

Holding the new baby had to be done ever so gently. Burping Jacob was an art; the trick was to pat his back hard enough to get a burp, yet gently enough not to break a bone. While other mothers celebrated their baby's first roll, for Tim and Lisa Cooper it was a cause for concern: "Gently, gently," they would chant.

"To win one's joy through struggle is better than to yield to melancholy." —André Maurois

Jacob loved the attention showered on him by adults. His vocabulary and maturity raced ahead of those of children his own age. "I think that Jacob has always been the center of attention and thrived on it," his mom says. "Jacob is so much more tuned in to adults than his peers because he's had to deal with so many life issues. His classmates don't know what it's like to have to decide whether to have an arm fixed or have a summer vacation. He does. We've made Jacob part of that decision-making process because it's such a huge part of his life."

The mature Jacob is learning to let go and be a kid. A frisky, Canine Companion named Nash signed on to walk the road to independence with Jacob.

Jacob was first introduced to the idea of a Canine Companion at age four when he was watching *Mister Rogers' Neighborhood* on TV. A young boy in a wheelchair appeared on the show, accompanied only by his service dog. No mom or dad, just the boy and his dog. Jacob thought it was neat and asked his mom if he could be like that boy some day. "I guess my interest in getting Jacob a dog was to provide him with a little more independence," Lisa says. She scribbled the phone number on a piece of paper and called Canine Companions for Independence.

A couple of years later the family made the decision to sign up for a dog. They were told the waiting list was about two years long; it would be three years before the Coopers got the call. "I ran up the stairs crying and asked him if he was ready to go," Lisa remembers. "Our basic rule before going on any big outing is that he must stay in one piece or we don't go. He was extra careful, but he said he didn't care if he was in a hip-to-toe cast, he was going anyway."

In February 2001 Jacob, his mom, and his grandmother packed their bags and headed for training at CCI north central campus in Delaware, Ohio. Joy Brownfield has been her grandson's full-time attendant at school since kindergarten, so she needed to be trained, too.

Lisa remembers being scared when she first saw Nash. He was huge and outweighed her son by at least twenty pounds. But he turned out to be a very gentle dog, and he knew how to be careful around Jacob. He crawled up to Jacob and rolled over to get a tummy rub. Puppy love; perfect partners.

One of his classmates, an older man from Canada, befriended Jacob, and the two laughed a lot. Jacob liked listening to the man with a college degree, a good job, a wife, and children.

Jacob's parents always told him his life could be anything he wanted and he believed them. But life was getting tougher the older he got; so many things didn't make sense. "The turmoil of being ten really hit him; in some ways he's so much older than others his age, but in other ways he's much younger," says Lisa. "Jacob isn't as independent; he can't run down the block and play or take off on his bicycle like other kids his age." His parents have spent a lifetime teaching him that nobody does everything by himself or herself; everybody needs help from time to time.

Jacob is different. Not less and not more. Just different.

And he's okay with that, most of the time. Jacob knows about roadblocks and about people who won't take the time to understand that he's a complete person. But for every one of those people, there are five who will take the time to understand and appreciate his differences.

Nash does. Jacob's mom is amazed at the deep connection the two have developed over the past year, adding that Nash can read Jacob better than she can. "When Jacob's not feeling well and I'm nagging him, Nash won't move," she says. "I have to make him get up and eat or go outside. He just wants to be right by Jacob all the time."

Life with Nash was the topic of a CCI graduation speech given by Jacob a year after his own graduation. He talked about the friendship that had grown, the tough times the two faced as a team, and the happy times when they played, then napped. "I hope you love your dog as much as I love my dog," he said at the end of his talk, then whispered a thank you to CCI for inviting him to speak. Jacob left the stage; his audience was left in tears, happy tears.

Nash's puppy raisers have Jacob's gratitude, too:

❤

Dear Bob and Jane,

Thank you for raising Nash. He's the best dog in the world. I can tell that you raised him with a lot of love and patience because that's what he shows me every day.

I'm glad CCI picked Nash for me because all of us are a perfect fit. Without Nash, I would never have known both of you.

This is really neat, my brother and I taught him a new trick. He can now give us a high five. I'm praying for both of you to have long, healthy lives so you can give someone else the same gift you gave me, a perfect friend.

Love always,
Jacob and Nash

But ask Jacob's mom about the biggest impact Nash has made in her young son's life and you might be surprised. "Jacob came to us and said he loves being invisible," Lisa says. "People notice Nash, not Jacob's wheelchair, and it's wonderful." Jacob told her that all the staring was constant wherever he went; he tried to get used to it, but it wasn't easy. Especially from other kids who have questions on their lips and a mom's hand pulling on an ear to reprimand them. "Now they go right for Nash," Jacob says, adding, "They don't even see me, and I like that a lot. I love it."

Nash has helped strengthen the bond between Jacob and his older brother, Tyler, too. Tyler says he can't wait until Jacob is older so the three of them can go out and "do their own thing."

"I would never have guessed it," Lisa says. "Going through the training—it was exhausting, and then I had to come home and teach the rest of the family what to do. But everything just fell into place. It's all working."

nash

Service Teams

"Dogs are an extension of us,
the part that is the very best
of what humans are capable of being."

Service Team   This team consists of an adult or adolescent with physical disabilities who works with a Canine Companion to extend his or her abilities and utilizes the dog to perform physical tasks such as pulling a wheelchair and retrieving dropped items.

New Beginnings

Call him Danger, Nick Danger. In 1995, a broken neck left the tough athlete paralyzed. The frustration, anguish, and physical pain he endured in the weeks following his accident were, in his words, "excruciating and endless."

That was then, this is now. These days, the handsome sportscaster-writer sits tall in his wheelchair, working hard to make a difference in the lives of people who are newly injured. He and his blonde sidekick, Rica, hang out at a place called Dangerwood. This Sherwood Forest—like Web site (www.survivingparalysis.com), where he and a band of followers exchange information, helps other quads navigate the murky waters of health and hope. No lectures here, just healthy doses of reality. Fact: Your life will never be the same. Fact: Turning things around is more than you can accomplish on your own.

"In life, what sometimes appears to be the end is really a new beginning." —Unknown

He tells it this way:

A man falls into a hole and is trapped. A priest walks by, and the man calls out for help. The priest sees him, writes a prayer on a piece of paper and drops it into the hole, then walks on. A doctor strolls by, and seeing that the man is in need of help, writes a prescription, drops it into the hole, and continues on his journey.

Finally, an old friend walks by and sees his buddy in distress. He stops, looks down into the hole, and then, to the amazement of the man in the hole, jumps down. The first man cries out, "You idiot, now we're BOTH stuck in the hole!"

"Yes," says the friend, "but I KNOW the way out."

Nick, whose real name is Steve Crowder, admits that he's had his share of hard hits in life, one that nearly did him in and another that put him on the sidelines when he thought his luck in the game of life was finally changing for the better. The first was his 1995 accident; the second was when he thought he had lost his chance to have a canine partner named Rica. Turns out, she had to jump into the hole to show *him* the way out.

"The year 2000 ended on a slightly down note," Nick wrote in a Christmas letter to friends. That November, his name came up on the waiting list to get a Canine Companion. He lasted the first four days, but a bizarre injury to his shoulder forced him to drop out.

A couple of hours before his first of two visits to the emergency room, Nick had been matched with a beautiful and energetic golden retriever named Rica. The second trip to the emergency room thrust Nick into something of a twilight zone, and he was unable to return to team training.

He says he dealt with the loss of Rica the way he had dealt with the loss of so many things since his accident: He shut down and put on a tough-guy act, veiling his disappointment with humor. His rehearsed line went something like this: "Oh sure, it would have been great, she's a terrific dog. But the fact is, when I dream at night, it's about girls, not a dog." But he was really hurting inside, he later admitted to a friend.

Then in February 2001, he got a call. THE call. CCI had an opening for one more graduate trainee. Would he be interested? It meant starting over—new teammates, new trainers, new dogs.

No pain or injury could have stopped the young man from completing the entire two-week course. He took the necessary precautions to assure there would be no repeat of the previous injuries that forced him to drop out.

He showed up not knowing that Rica was slated for the same class. "I couldn't believe my eyes when she was led into the room," he says. Although the two had spent only a couple of hours as a team in November, Nick knew it was a match. They clicked. Everyone saw it, both in the dog's eyes and in Nick's heart. The two were paired for another try, and Nick never took his eyes off her. On graduation day, she stood by his side while Nick Danger spoke of his gratitude, love, and plans for the two of them. And there wasn't a dry eye in the auditorium as Nick put his wheelchair in gear and moved forward with Rica at his side.

In the next six months, Nick underwent two painful surgeries and bought a house on a golf course. Contractors took five weeks to alter the space to suit Nick's lifestyle needs, and friends helped him move in on schedule.

Looking back on 2001, Nick says he felt truly blessed. The journey had been long and hard, needlessly complicated at times, and he knew it was up to him to do something about it. And so he created Dangerwood, a vehicle to express his gratitude by reaching out to others the way people have reached out to him. In the winter, he and Rica are courtside, announcing basketball games for his alma mater, the University of California at San Diego. Then it's baseball in the spring.

Life is precious to Nick Danger. "And teaming with Rica has given me the independence to be able to indulge in it by living and enjoying myself since becoming a quadriplegic," he says, adding, "There is so much that I enjoy doing that I almost never think about the things that I can no longer do." He is currently writing a novel and intends to finish it within a year.

Service dogs are trained to respond to sixty commands. At bottom left, Rica opens a door for Nick.

On graduation day, she stood by his side while Nick Danger spoke of his gratitude, love, and plans for the two of them.

Work's the Thing

shelby

Shelby is twelve years old going on eighty-four. But there's nothing retiring about the golden retriever—not in her attitude, aptitude, or ambition. In fact, speaking the "R" word in her presence is like waving a red flag at a bull. Same difference—both snort and get feisty.

These days, the old girl is working hard at playing more and teaching her partner, Sally Simcoe, to do the same. Take life too seriously and you will lose yourself, the grinning dog barks. Shelby's nods and nudges are the dog's way of telling her partner that it's time to stop and sniff the roses, play some ball, and maybe roll in the grass. "She reminds me to take care of myself," Sally says. "I will get engrossed in something and forget about the time. Then I feel this nose poking me, and when I pay attention to her, I realize that my shoulders are all tense."

Sally, a self-described Type A personality, works for Hewlett Packard in northern California, developing training programs for its computer-repair staff. She loves her work and would rather play—uh, *work* at the computer than do almost anything else. For as long as she can remember, Sally says, she has searched for projects to challenge both her mind and her body.

"The fun of being alive is realizing that you have a talent; use it every day so it grows stronger." —Lou Centlivre

Polio ravaged Sally's young body just one year before Salk discovered a vaccine to halt the disease. In the years that followed her illness, the muscles in her body weakened, and Sally found a wheelchair useful. More than useful, she says; it gave her the opportunity to play sports. In her twenties, Sally wheeled her way to a gold medal at the Toronto Paralympics.

Sally says she thought often about having a Canine Companion for Independence in the years before she was partnered with Shelby. "I first heard about CCI in 1984 when I attended the Abilities Expo in Los Angeles," she says. "I watched a demonstration and thought it was pretty cool but didn't think I was disabled enough for a dog. But I did keep the possibility in the back of my mind for somewhere down the road."

Sally married Kent Simcoe in 1987, and the two took a trip to the Abilities Expo that same year. Again, she watched a canine-graduate team demonstration and liked what she saw. But still, she didn't think she could qualify for a dog, so didn't bother to inquire.

Later that year, she accepted a new job at Hewlett Packard. And that's where fate intervened. Among her new co-workers was a CCI puppy raiser who brought her four-legged trainee to work with her every day. Sally talked to the woman about the role the dog would play after she grew up and was completely trained. And for so many days, in so many little ways, Sally grew to appreciate just how much a CCI dog could do to help her become more independent. The puppy raiser encouraged Sally to sign up for a canine helpmate.

In the spring of 1991, Sally filled out the required paperwork and submitted her request for a service dog at CCI's main campus in Santa Rosa, California. There were more interviews, reams of applications to be filled out, letters of reference and referrals to be obtained. In the end, her name was placed on a list that put the waiting time at approximately two years.

Fifteen months later, she got the call. She was invited to train and qualify for a Canine Companion. Graduate applicants are required to attend a fourteen-day training program and pass both written and public-access tests. Sally put in the required long

hours of hard work, smiling as her Type A personality kicked into gear.

She was teamed with a series of dogs, but she figured Kaufman would probably go home with her. Eerie, she said to herself, Kaufman's picture had been taped to her office cubicle months before she'd even met the dog. "Kaufman was featured in a Hewlett Packard company newsletter about employees and their volunteer work," she says. "HP has been a big CCI supporter for years, and I hoped the trainers would match us since Kaufman was familiar with the HP office."

Then Sally met Shelby. Both had long, curly tresses. One night at play, people teased Sally that they couldn't tell them apart from the back. The next day they were teamed for training, and the rest is history. Perfect match, the trainers said, noting that both had outgoing personalities, both sparkled, and both would rather work than play. They were simpatico.

Shelby has never been called on to save Sally's life. But with Shelby by her side, Sally is living a satisfying and independent life.

And Shelby has turned her nurturing nature to Kent. A partly paralyzed leg put him temporarily in Sally's extra wheelchair, so Shelby pitched in to help make his life easier, too. "I think Shelby still thinks she's a puppy," Sally says. "She likes being needed, so when we talk about retiring her, Shelby just perks up and gets busy doing something. It's not time, not just yet." Maybe soon, though. These treasured canines usually retire after eight to ten years of service, depending on their health.

Sally knows that life without Shelby would be difficult. She got a taste of what it was like four years ago when Shelby was sidelined with a knee injury. Coming home tired from work, Sally didn't have a second pair of paws to do so many little things that make her life easier. Shelby was at the veterinarian's office, recovering from biopsy surgery. Still groggy from the anesthesia, Shelby heard the clang of something hitting the floor and responded immediately. She got up off the bed, walked over to the dropped object, then picked it up and handed it to the veterinary technician. He was impressed. "That's her work ethic," Sally says. "In her mind, it's 'Yeah, I don't feel good, but somebody needs me.' That's how she responds."

The two have partied in matching silk-and-sequin outfits for charity galas, dressed up as Easter bunnies to pass out candy eggs, and even played Little Red Riding Hood at Halloween. Once, they had matching burgundy pedicures and manicures. Dress up Shelby and watch her strut—she loves being the center of attention, according to Sally.

Every Sunday, Sally, Kent, and Shelby sit at the front of the church wearing choir robes. Sally sings soprano, Kent sings baritone, and Shelby—Shelby snores in dreamy whimpers and whines. Shelby has the pastor's blessing to sleep through the entire service, sermon and all.

Shelby, whose real name is Ashelby, has also served as CEC (chief executive canine) of Ashelby Pro-Bono Productions, a nonprofit business organized solely to record graduations and special engagements on videotape at the CCI northwest

A family portrait: Kent, Sally, and Shelby Simcoe. Although Shelby is officially Sally's dog, she helped Kent, too, when he was temporarily disabled.

regional campus. And then there are guest appearances on a Bay Area pet network— strictly pro bono. Now and then, Shelby still stars in public-service announcements, including one for SOUL (Source of Unconditional Love) at Mercy Health Care in Sacramento.

The caring canine serves as a magnet, bringing out the metal in people. Even the shy and awkward reach out to touch Shelby's spirit. "We can spot grumpy and frowning people walking down the halls at work," Sally says. "In an instant, the moment their eyes meet Shelby's eyes, she lightens their moods. She comes by with a ball in her mouth ready to play and people realize that life isn't as bad as it seems."

Then there's the humor Shelby brings out in people. When Sally's mother-in-law died, she and Shelby flew to Loveland, Colorado, to be near Kent and offer their support. The three of them, plus Kent's brother, Terry, rode an elevator to the second floor at Fort Collins Courthouse. When the door opened, the sight of Shelby shocked a woman waiting to board the elevator. Always the clown, Terry explained, "We brought our attorney. She's a real bitch."

Humor helps—maybe not with this particular lady— but it made Kent laugh, and that made Sally happy. The lesson: You just can't take life too seriously.

Weaver's Journey

Clad in white tie and tails, Weaver Hollenstein sauntered into the cruise ship's formal dining room, aware that every eye was focused on him. He shook the captain's hand, then took his assigned seat *under* the table.

Weaver, a Canine Companion, was on his retirement cruise with partner Tom Hollenstein. The three days of mournful merriment off the coast of Mexico were meant as a *muchas gracias* for nearly eleven years of faithful service. Not to mention the fun, of which there was lots. "Weaver was such a character, he deserved to retire in style," Tom says. And so he did, for a while. But retirement didn't suit the dutiful dog, as his partner would soon learn.

Tom was partnered with Weaver two years after a bicycle accident left him paralyzed. He and a friend were racing up and down the slopes on a construction site when a five-foot trench caught him by surprise, twisting his body and breaking his neck. At age twenty-four, he found his life taking a wrong-way detour down a one-way street. He knew from the moment he hit the ground that his body was badly broken. He thought he was dead; he felt as if he were up in the clouds looking down. He prayed to God to let him live.

"I'm a little wounded, but I am not slain; I will lay me down to bleed a while. Then I'll rise and fight again." —John Dryden

While he was recuperating in the hospital, rehabilitation therapists took Tom to an Abilities Expo in Los Angeles. A Canine Companions for Independence team was there to demonstrate the advantages of working with a service dog. He liked the idea of a canine partner, but it would be another two years before he would meet and

With the wind in his face, jowls flapping in the breeze, weekends for Weaver were wonderful.

be matched with Weaver. In the meantime, he worked to get his body strong again and made peace with his new life. He completed his training as a private detective and was hired to track missing persons and do asset research by telephone.

But it didn't feel right. He didn't want to work inside an office glued to a telephone all day any more than he wanted to continue living in his parents' home. He wanted more independence and knew he would have to figure out a way to get it for himself. A few months later, he received a call from CCI and signed on for the fall 1987 training class.

Tom and Weaver had each other's number from the first day they met. The big yellow Lab with doe

eyes worked his magic on Tom and vice versa. They were inseparable, as time and trials would prove.

Tom laughs, remembering the first and last time he went on a trip and left Weaver at home. Quarantine restrictions made traveling with a canine impossible. The day before the trip, out came the suitcase and in went everything for the man and nothing for the dog. Weaver sniffed the leather bag and looked downcast. He knew that wherever the man and the suitcase were going, he wasn't going with them. And so he sulked. Then he vomited on the floor next to the travel bag.

While he was traveling, Tom called home every few hours to check on Weaver, only to learn that the dog was still pouting, not eating, and generally grumpy. And life wasn't easy on the Oahu side of the Pacific Ocean, either. That weekend, Tom learned just how much independence Weaver afforded him and that he needed Weaver just as much as the dog needed him.

When Tom got home, he bought Weaver his own traveling bag, and the next time one suitcase came out, so did the other. He packed his clothes and toiletries; then he packed Weaver's food, toys, and a blanket. Where one went, the other went, too.

A one-time amateur-circuit surfer, Tom learned to water-ski the year after his injury. A special ski rig allowed him to hit the water and play in the white waves stirring in the boat's wake. He fell into the water face down and held his breath until a water buddy turned the ski skyward. Weaver sat on the boat with his full attention on the skier. The minute Tom fell, Weaver would let out an alert bark that sent friends overboard on a mission. With the wind in his face, jowls flapping in the breeze, weekends for Weaver were wonderful.

Tom's life was back on track, thanks to Weaver. "He gave me back the independence I never thought I would have," he says. "He gave me the confidence to make the move out of my parents' house and into my own apartment. And he helped me get my first outside job."

When Tom dropped his apartment keys, Weaver retrieved the keys and put them in his hand. When a muscle spasm twisted his body, knocking him onto the floor, it was Weaver who got the cordless phone so he could call for help. Little things, lots of things all added up to a life of independent living.

While at a dog show, he and Weaver passed a Science Diet pet food promotion booth and stopped to talk. The representative, impressed with how well Tom and Weaver worked as a team, offered him a part-time job. As marketing representatives they called on pet stores and spent their days talking with people and selling Science Diet. A natural at sales, Tom moved from that job to a career in medical supplies.

Ten years came and went; it was time to think about retiring Weaver and accepting a successor Canine Companion. But first, Tom wanted to give Weaver a proper send-off, so he booked a cruise. After they got home, he folded Weaver's blue cape and put it in the closet, officially releasing him from work duties.

Another dog came into their lives but didn't last long. Between Weaver's hurt looks, Tom's guilt, and the other dog's unwillingness to play second fiddle, the match didn't fit. "I decided to return the dog and not get another dog until Weaver took his last breath," Tom says. "Weaver gave me back my life after the accident. He forced me to take the plunge and go for a job. I felt I owed it to him to see him happy all the way until his last day."

Tom says that when he brought Weaver's blue cape out of retirement, the dog wagged his tail so hard it knocked over some furniture. It was clear that Weaver's heart and will to work were as strong as ever. Tom says he made a commitment to give up a little of his own independence and work at Weaver's slower pace.

When Weaver ached from arthritis, Tom found an acupuncturist to ease his pain. Weaver made the effort to get into the van when it was time to work, but was content to stay behind while Tom called on clients alone.

Some months later, Weaver suffered his first stroke, and Tom prepared for the worst. The dog rebounded within a few weeks and was back as strong as he was before his stroke. Tom decided it was time to give Weaver extra liberties; he put him in the van and drove to Boston Market for a chicken dinner. Later that week, the two went to Ben and Jerry's for a Chunky Monkey ice-cream cone.

Seven months later, another stroke paralyzed Weaver's body. "I figured it was time to make the one decision I had always hoped I'd never have to make," Tom says. He bundled Weaver in a blanket, and a friend put him in the back seat of the van. But the veterinarian had good news for Tom. He told him that he should give Weaver time to recover; he was pretty sure the dog would rebound. Nine days later, the old Weaver was back ready to work and play. The two went back to their schedule of weekend water-ski trips and outings in the park. And Weaver was fine, for a while.

But time was running out and Tom knew it. He called the Southwest Regional Center and asked them keep an eye out for a dog to follow in Weaver's footsteps. "I got a telephone call a week later from a trainer there who said the perfect dog for me had become available," Tom says. "We drove to Oceanside so Weaver could meet Hiley." Tom says he rolled his chair into a huge room where a dozen dogs were training. His eyes were drawn to a small yellow Labrador/golden retriever cross. He remembers thinking that he hoped this was the dog they had picked for him. And it was.

Weaver met Hiley, and Tom is convinced that the two dogs communicated; Weaver accepted Hiley as his successor. It would be okay for him to leave; his friend would be in good company. From that day, Weaver surrendered to age and ill health. It was time for him to go.

Tom knew the signs; he knew it was time to make the decision he never wanted to make. He had hoped that Weaver would die peacefully in his sleep, but it wasn't going to happen that way. "I told him it was okay to let go, that I'd be all right," he says. "Then I called the vet and asked him to come to my home. I took Weaver for one last Chunky Monkey cone, but he didn't get excited. I knew he wasn't having fun anymore."

The night he died, Tom told Weaver how very grateful he was for having him in his life. The vet injected a lethal dose into Weaver's leg while Tom held him in his arms, whispering over and over how much he loved him. He held the dog long after the vet said Weaver was gone. "I wanted to make sure that the last words he heard were mine and that he knew how very much he was loved," Tom says. He felt a little bit of peace flow through the room that night. There was even more peace the next morning when he woke up. "I didn't have to wonder in my heart if Weaver was trying to get up off the floor to come and say a last goodbye to me. He died in my arms, knowing that I would be okay. And I knew that he would be okay."

Hiley, another miracle dog, arrived the next day; not to replace Weaver, but to continue the work he had started.

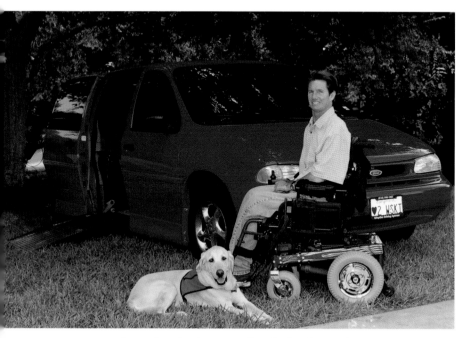

Even when they're on vacation, Canine Companions are on the job. Tom and Hiley often go on jaunts together.

Cruising through Life

bahrt

Bahrt moves with a smoothness and sureness that get him noticed; catch his gaze and you'll find the window that looks into the calm of his soul.

It was like that the first time Bill Roth met Bahrt, back in the summer of '95 when the busy executive took a long-needed break to see if they could work as a team. The two personalities meshed. It seemed as if Bill needed Bahrt as much as Bahrt needed him. Bill, diagnosed with muscular dystrophy at birth, was increasingly losing his struggle for independence and needed a Canine Companion to help him. He and Bahrt graduated after two weeks of intense training at the Canine Companions for Independence campus in Delaware, Ohio.

Three weeks later, Bill and wife, Peach, were packing their bags for an Alaskan cruise, a trip the successful corporate boss had won for working so hard. Bill wasn't sure Bahrt was ready for a sea trip, but CCI trainers convinced the couple that the dog could do it. And so they packed a third bag, this one with chew toys and a tux.

Bill's all-work-and-no-play world was about to be turned right side up.

"Man cannot live by bread alone.

He must have peanut butter." —Brother Dave Gardner

They arrived at the airport early, checked in, and cleared security with an hour to spare. Bahrt, Bill, and Peach were bumped up to first class. Bahrt slurped bottled water from a United Airlines silver bowl while Bill sipped whiskey from a crystal glass. Both of them schmoozed and snoozed during the long trip from Ohio to Vancouver, British Columbia.

Peach smiled. It had been twenty years since she and her husband had been on a vacation, and this one was starting out on a grand note. Peach marveled at how much the dog's easy-going manner had rubbed off on her husband.

The plane landed on time, and they hailed a cab for the trip to the docks. Peach says you'd have thought a movie star had strolled into the bon voyage gala instead of Bahrt. The red carpet was already down; Peach swears that if it hadn't been, they'd have found one and rolled it out just for him. Everywhere you looked, there were smiles aimed at the man and his Canine Companion. People got even giddier when they found out that Bahrt was traveling with them.

More people poured out of buses, taxis, and limousines until the dock was standing room only. Champagne glasses clinked and the reception line formed at the right to greet both the ship's officers *and* Bahrt. Bill made the introductions and says if dogs could shrug, Bahrt would have been working his shoulders nonstop at all the commotion. As it was, the Lab stretched out his paw on command and shook enough hands to get him elected president. Finally, Bahrt moved under the nearest table and took a nap until the crew of the *Amsterdam* blasted the horn. It was time to get on board.

Bill put his electric wheelchair into high gear and found a patch of green grass to toilet Bahrt before making his way to the ship. It wasn't until the next day that Bill would realize just how important his decision had been to head for one last pit stop for Bahrt.

They made their way to the cabin and discovered a tray of chocolate truffles and a bottle of good whiskey to welcome their arrival. A huge bag of dog food leaned against the table legs, big enough for a week of breakfasts, lunches, dinners, and even an occasional midnight buffet. Sweet.

The first night out, Bill found the casino and settled in to, as he put it, "give the ship some more of my money." Bahrt liked to sit at Bill's side for hours on end while Bill played poker and sipped whiskey-flavored colas. After a couple of drinks, the dog poked Bill on the leg with his nose and gave him a look that was nothing short of a lecture. They left with some of the ship's money in Bill's pocket.

On the way back to the room, Bill took Bahrt to the designated area on the "poop" deck so the dog could do his business. Nothing. Bahrt, it seemed, wouldn't think of soiling the ship's deck any more than he would use the cabin as a toilet. Bill was worried; they would be at sea for at least another twelve hours or so.

The next morning, Bill offered Bahrt a bowl of water and the dog lapped it up. Then he took him up to the game deck and played fetch with a tennis ball until the dog's bladder surrendered. Whew! Evenings, Bill's brother Richard jogged around the deck with Bahrt at his side, and they didn't stop until the dog toileted.

And that became the routine at sea. They'd fill the dog with water and play ball or jog until the dog toileted. Bahrt would get this sheepish look on his face, and his eyes would pan the area to make sure no one was looking. The good news was that most days the ship docked at places where there were acres of green August grass for Bahrt to sniff out his special spot.

Bill admits that he was apprehensive about taking Bahrt on the cruise, but that when they were just one day out of Vancouver he was sure he had made the right decision. The dog had the manners of a country gentleman's best friend. Bahrt's finest hours were when he donned his tux for fancy affairs. His demeanor was as genteel as his finery was fancy.

Bahrt posed for lots of photographs; almost everyone wanted his or her picture taken with the canine celebrity. He'd hear the word "cheese" and his chin would turn up just as the flash went off.

Good dog.

The dog had the manners of a country gentleman's best friend. Bahrt's finest hours were when he donned his tux for fancy affairs.

Well, "good dog" except for the time a crewman donned a polar-bear suit and growled a friendly welcome as passengers disembarked at Ketchikan. Bahrt wanted a piece of the bear's hide when he looked cross-eyed at Bill. The dog bolted for the bear, and it took all the strength that Bill and Richard could muster to keep him from dragging the chair down the ramp. Bahrt has never reared his protective side since, Bill says, adding that the dog is gentle, attentive, well behaved, and never disruptive.

The dog even kept his cool when an inebriated woman cornered Bill and lectured him on the "cruelty of keeping this dog on a leash to be at your beck and call." The dog looked up at Bill the whole time with a mournful mug. Bill thought it was pity for the woman, but it was pain. Her left foot was planted on the dog's tail the whole time she was screaming at Bill.

The best moments for Bill and Peach were watching the ice crack and tumble free during the afternoon when the ship sat anchored in Glacier Bay. The afternoon was warm by Alaskan standards—sweatshirt-and-windbreaker weather. The huge hulks of ice would shatter and fall into the bay. The Roths never missed a viewing, thanks to Bahrt's keen hearing. They watched his ears perk up, then followed his eyes; it was, they say, like watching the world through the innocence and wonder of a child's eyes. Trips off the ship were the best times for Bahrt; he would bury his nose, then fall to the ground and make an angel dog in the snow.

Not a bad moment on the trip—not for Bill, Peach, or Bahrt. They came home rested and ready to tackle the world. The cabin steward, a young boy who was terrified of dogs, made Bahrt a little Dutch hat as a souvenir. He dropped to his knees and gave the huge Labrador a hug, brushing away a tear from his cheek. Bahrt had won him over by letting him warm up to him at his own pace. He waited for the boy to come to him, and then he melted his heart.

There have been no more ocean trips or vacations anywhere. But Bahrt refuses to let Bill work twelve-hour days; eight hours is tops. Saturdays are filled with rock concerts, college ball games, and car races. Sundays are for sleeping in and snuggling up to Bill.

The two follow the philosophy that has served them well, something that Bahrt brought with him when he came to live with the Roths: Neither man nor dog can live by bread alone. He must have peanut butter.

All That Yaz

A cavernous voice pierced through the fog of anesthesia like a ship pushing through the seas off Antarctica. Life, as Tim Daynes knew it, had been smashed into as many pieces as an ice-cutting ship leaves in its wake.

He heard the same voice call his name and deliver a sentence of what could only be described as hell on earth. "Tim," the doctor's voice began, "your neck is broken and you are a quadriplegic. You will never walk again or be able to feed yourself. You can never play sports, and you will never have children. You must just learn to ask

"Start by doing what's necessary, then what's possible, and suddenly you are doing the impossible." —Saint Francis of Assisi

someone for help for the rest of your life."

The sixteen-year-old high school athlete lay in a hospital bed, devastated in both body and soul. In the blink of a dive gone wrong, his neck had hit an underwater sandbar. Tim's young life catapulted from the carefree waters of Utah's Lake Powell to the confines of a battered and broken body.

He spent the next six months relearning the simple tasks he had once mastered as a toddler and began the arduous task of rebuilding his life one step at a time. Although he couldn't walk, Tim learned to stand on his own two feet. He took the hand he had been dealt, put on a poker face, and got back into the game.

He constantly upped the ante, challenging the doctors' prognosis. He loved to beat them at their own game. Best of all, the young man learned to laugh again.

He was healing; but his return to his old Salt Lake City high school opened new wounds. "I can't begin to tell you how painful that time was for me," he says, looking back thirteen years ago. Meeting his peers again, this time in a wheelchair, was tough. Suddenly, people he had known for most of his life turned and walked the other way when they saw him wheel down the hallways. Other students didn't acknowledge his presence. They literally talked over his head.

But Tim was determined to graduate with his class even though he had lost nearly a full year of study. And he did it; he even figured out a way to cope emotionally. He turned to humor. "I ran for senior class vice president with the slogan 'Roll with Tim,' and I won," he says.

But a combination of choices had made his first year as a quad very hard. In addition to returning to school and taking on a double workload, Tim refused electric wheels and instead opted for a manual chair. His muscles balked at the heavy demands. It would take time to get strong again but Tim couldn't wait, and so he pushed his body daily to new limits.

On weekend nights, out with friends, he said he felt like a charity case. They would drop him off at home around 10 o'clock and then go back out for

Ehreth is as energetic as Yaz was laid back. And he loves to put on his

more fun. "They felt very uncomfortable around me; just didn't know what to say, I guess," Tim says, but that made it hurt even more. He wanted his friends back. He wanted things to be the way they had been before his diving accident. It just didn't happen.

Graduation came and went, and Tim headed off to college. "That last year of high school, when I was feeling so rejected, I learned that I needed to find new friends. I felt I had no other choice; you either find ways to keep moving forward or stay where you are and be miserable."

Tim believes that what really helped get him moving was his ability to nurture his sense of humor. He felt more accepted when he could make people laugh; people just felt more comfortable around him.

He began to accept speaking engagements, and the more he talked, the more confidence he found inside himself. He talked openly about his limitations and challenges and then turned the tables on his audience. "Everybody has limitations and challenges, it's just that mine are obvious," he says. "I asked people what they were doing to make a difference in their

backpack to go to work. Tim calls him his overachiever.

179

own lives and in the lives of others."

Summer ended and it was time to head off to the University of Utah, but not before acquiring a new friend to tag along. Tim met Yaz, a ninety-pound golden retriever/Labrador mix, and was matched with him during two weeks of training at CCI's Southwest Regional Center in Oceanside, California. The service dog was trained to help a person with a disability become more independent, something Tim would need to strike out on his own. Suddenly, everything changed. "Yaz helped me gain a good deal of independence. He was able to pull my chair up some steep hills, get around campus, and pick up things I dropped."

But the best part was the doors he opened. They didn't come with handles or knobs; these doors were social barriers. "Having Yaz with me all the time made all the difference in the world," Tim says. "Without Yaz, I'm sure I would be a different person today—more withdrawn and less trusting. I don't think I would have this sense of humor that has helped me survive. Yaz made my wheelchair less threatening, and people weren't hesitant about approaching me. People focused on the dog, came up and shared stories about their own pets, and then we went on to talk about other things. Yaz was the ultimate icebreaker."

When Yaz walked, it was more of a prance. Tim describes it as the prance of a thoroughbred that has just won the Kentucky Derby. "But he never moved fast; in fact, he was a little lazy," Tim smiles. "I never had to worry about excitable greetings. And when he wanted someone to stay, he'd sit on his or her shoes.

> When Yaz walked, it was more of a prance. Tim describes it as the prance of a thoroughbred that has just won the Kentucky Derby.

It was tough to get up and go with ninety pounds of dog on your toes."

Yaz was there when Tim graduated from the University of Utah. He was there when Tim met, wooed, and proposed to Karen. The two were married in 1998; Yaz was the ring bearer. He pranced down the aisle with a pink bone pillow, made to match the bridesmaid dresses. The rings were anchored with ribbons. The pillow, teeth marks and all, is a family treasure. Yaz died a year later.

Losing Yaz broke Tim's heart. "I was reading e-mails from friends expressing their sympathy and feelings of loss," he says, "when all of a sudden this yellow ladybug landed on my left arm on the place where I still have some feeling. The next morning, I'm at the breakfast bar eating a bowl of cereal when I see the yellow ladybug right next to me. It had to be the same one. I've never seen a yellow one before; didn't know they existed. It was eerie. It made me think of Yaz and smile."

Later that day, Tim was going through his closet to find a framed picture of Yaz to give to his father. He found his dad's favorite photo, put it into a bag, and drove to his dad's office. "I pulled the photo out of the bag and handed it to my father. The same ladybug was on the picture," Tim says, admitting to chills.

Maybe it was the spirit of Yaz, coming home to tell Tim he was all right and was still looking after him. Maybe it was Tim's need for comfort that made him notice a yellow ladybug. No matter, it did the job. Father and son laughed and told Yaz stories.

In 1999 Tim was matched with a successor Canine

Karen and Tim
Daynes with Yaz.

Companion named Ehreth. Ehreth is ten pounds lighter and 180 degrees different from Yaz in personality. He is the same mix of Labrador and golden retriever, but there the similarities end. Ehreth is as energetic as Yaz was laid back. Yaz was always up for a nap, but Ehreth rarely sleeps. And he loves to put on his backpack to go to work. Tim calls him his over-achiever.

Looking back on his diving accident, Tim takes responsibility for making some bad choices that day. "We all make bad choices from time to time," he says,

adding, "The real challenge is never to give up. That and to take the time to make a difference in other people's lives, that's what's important.

Fun is important, too. Fun, spelled s-k-y-d-i-v-i-n-g. Not so risky for someone who is already a quadriplegic, Tim laughs. The idea is to have as much fun as he can, despite the fact that his physical limitations are so great. "Sometimes I think this is crazy. I can't even pick up a pen off the floor, but then I laugh; you just have to laugh it off. And then go on to the next challenge."

Golden Rule

raven

The hospital light flickered, sending the nurse sprinting down the hallway to see who was in pain and how she could help. A stabbing pain raced up her right leg. Nothing more than a pulled muscle, or so she thought.

The days passed into weeks. The sharp ache increased in both intensity and intervals. Surgery was necessary, the doctors told Carolyn Edwards. She watched the operation and said the doctor did just fine; she didn't. A spinal headache relentlessly hammered her body for a week. The staff rescheduled her physical therapy and encouraged her to go home and rest.

Carolyn was talking to her mom when she heard her father's screams for help. Months before, he had suffered a stroke, and his daughter feared it was happening all over again. Carolyn rushed up the stairs, but something made her crumple into a withering pile of pain. Mystified, she went to bed and stayed there until she went to her therapy appointment the next day. Looking back, she says the only bright spot in all this was that her father had not suffered a stroke, after all.

"Pain is inevitable. Suffering is optional." —Anonymous

Time has passed since that autumn day in 1995, but the pain never has. Carolyn has figured out ways to live with the physical torment and not let it take over her life. Mind over matter, she says, adding that pain is unavoidable; suffering, however, is voluntary.

Carolyn has reflex sympathetic dystrophy, a syndrome that sometimes occurs following any type of trauma. Doctors don't know why it happens. It can take many forms, and the nerve pain is always intense.

Carolyn describes it as feeling as if someone were pouring hot coals over her leg.

The limb's circulation has become compromised, which, in turn, destroys muscles and bones. Carolyn's right leg rests permanently in an extended position that cannot be corrected by surgery. Another injury, perhaps even the surgery itself, could cause an increase in pain.

Fear, more than pain, haunts the woman who once loved to be surrounded by people. She and her husband have moved to an isolated area in the Blue Ridge Mountains of North Carolina, where their nearest neighbors are nearly a mile away.

bottom front teeth; ditto for him.

On graduation night, Carolyn's heart was filled with so much joy that it spilled out of her eyes in droplets. She lost a contact lens and couldn't see anything as she wheeled her way onstage to take his leash.

Raven is her hero, taking a backseat only to her husband, Wayne. The couple celebrated their thirty-seventh anniversary this year with their three children, Wayne, Candace, and Heather. Wayne has been her steel rod throughout the good times and the bad. He was the one who encouraged her to go back to

People laugh when they hear Raven's name; his moniker belies his golden fur.

Fear moved into her heart until a dog named Raven II chased it away. The Canine Companion has brought out the old Carolyn, and the two do what they can to make other people's hurt go away. Easy, she says, with Raven at her side as her security blanket.

Stares from strangers pushed Carolyn into a shell. She was reminded that she was different with every peering glance. With Raven, the stares are welcome because most of them are directed his way. Sometimes, she confesses, she actually forgets that she looks so different that she sticks out in a crowd. And when she does find herself feeling self-conscious, she rubs Raven's velvet head and her fears are soothed away.

People laugh when they hear Raven's name; his moniker belies his golden fur. Carolyn laughed the first time she met the golden retriever/Labrador mix. Raven just sauntered up and placed his huge jowls on her lap. Then he looked up and grinned; his eyes were mesmerizing. The more she got to know him, the better Carolyn understood that they were a matched set. Raven has a tendency to gain weight; ditto for her. Carolyn has a wide gap between her

school after their children were grown to get her nursing degree.

In the spring of 2001, the good times switched to turmoil. And this time, Wayne wouldn't be there to help her through the ordeal. A heart attack had claimed the life of a dear friend only the month before, and it looked as if the disease were about to claim another victim: Wayne.

The possibility of losing Wayne broke Carolyn's heart and spirit. He had always been there for her; he was the strong one. This time, she was determined to be there for him, with a little help from Raven. She says it was Raven who gave her the strength and stability she needed. "Dogs are an extension of us," she says, "the part that is the very best of what humans are capable of being." Raven, she insists, is an angel that God sent to walk with her through the darkest times and show her the way. Carolyn puts all her faith in God and believes in His plan, even when she doesn't understand it.

After hours in surgery, Wayne was moved to the intensive care unit at Carolina Medical Center in

Raven lending a paw in the garden.

Charlotte. He was there for three days, teetering between this life and the next. When the staff found Carolyn in the waiting room shortly after surgery, they were adamant that Raven come with her to see Wayne. "Thank God he was with me, otherwise I would have fallen out of my chair," she says. Carolyn thought she knew what to expect, but she wasn't prepared when she saw Wayne. The former registered nurse says she'd seen dead patients that looked healthier than her husband.

That night, Carolyn remembers feeling exhausted, frightened, and terribly alone. Her grown children would soon go back to their own lives, leaving her alone with the possibility of life without Wayne. "Raven smothered me with doggy kisses, snuggled so close, and let me know he was there for the both of us," she says. "Only someone who has a Canine Companion would understand how close a team becomes. Because of CCI's love, I knew I would never be alone and that I would have Raven's help to go on."

Once Wayne had been moved to the cardiac floor, Carolyn and Raven moved in, too. Carolyn watched her husband's face and the rows of flashing monitors from a recliner; Raven found an out-of-the-way spot behind the chair and settled in. Raven pulled her through the ordeal with enough love and strength to pull other devastated families through their intensive care traumas.

Raven and Carolyn made their way through the hospital corridors several times a day for food and bathroom breaks. Occasionally, family members vis-iting other patients would ask Carolyn to bring Raven inside for a visit. Carolyn never refused, not even in those early days when she wasn't sure if she was a wife or a widow. She knew how much she herself valued Raven's company and was willing to share it.

On one occasion, a woman begged Carolyn to bring the dog to visit her elderly mother, explaining that she missed her dog so much that she was making herself sick. "The mother loved Raven to death. We left her smiling," Carolyn says. Later, when the daughter found out that Carolyn's husband was a patient and in very serious condition, she apologized for taking up her time. "She thought we were the hospital's pet therapy team."

"In some ways, our relationship is closer than a marriage," Carolyn says. "I know this sounds funny, but I don't know any other way to describe how I feel about Raven. He is an extension of me, and sometimes it scares me how well he knows me. When we're apart, it feels like I've split myself up."

The dog has offered her the independence she craved; the two drove to Ohio by themselves to be with Carolyn's daughter when her fourth grandson was born. Carolyn says she wouldn't even have considered making that trip without Raven.

Wayne recovered from his heart attack, and he, Carolyn, and Raven have taken four cruises so far. Carolyn and her four-legged best friend tour the ship while Wayne goes off to do other activities. Raven's presence gives her the freedom she had remembered and cherished. 🐾

raven

flair
A Friend in Need

Ron Cote is a "glass-is-always-half-full" kind of guy who searches for the best in people and seldom comes up short. His laugh is infectious; a hiccupping melody that spreads around a room as fast as whipped butter melts on hot flapjacks.

His life had taken so many unexpected twists and turns that he felt prepared to make the best of the worst. He'd done it before, lots of times since his body had been invaded by an insidious disease that claimed his muscles one by one. The doctors explained his future using long Latin names; they all spelled out the same fate. Eventually, Ron was told, his balance, speech, and motor skills would run down.

He traded his chef's hat for less strenuous work; his body was aging faster than the passing years. The time came for Ron to reach out for help, and when he did, he found Canine Companions for Independence. Ron was matched with a feisty golden retriever who answered to the moniker Flair. After two weeks of team training, Ron and Flair were like peanut butter and jelly. Both are good, but they're better together.

"Believe, when you are most unhappy, that there is something for you to do in the world. So long as you can sweeten another's pain, life is not in vain." —Helen Keller

Mornings started the same, always. Ron grabbed a cane in one hand and Flair's leash in the other, and the two went out for their morning stroll. They walked along the same path, stopping to chat or tell a joke and laugh.

The laughter stopped one September morning when they were ambushed by two pit bulls. The dogs knocked Ron off his feet and jumped over his sprawled body.

Flair turned to protect him and found herself sandwiched between the angry dogs. They went for her neck, pulled her off her feet, and began shaking her. Ron screamed, Flair whimpered. Ron wept, Flair lay silent.

The dogs were tearing at Flair's neck when a handful of strangers rushed to the rescue. One man threw a pail of water on the dogs while two others pulled the dogs off Flair. More help came, and the dogs turned tail and ran off. Ron knelt over his dog. Both were in deep shock.

Flair was rushed to Pacific Animal Hospital in Oceanside, California. Ron was incoherent; trauma had rendered his speech useless. Hospital staff recognized Flair's CCI tags and questioned Ron about his dog. He asked them to call Barbara Richman, a CCI puppy raiser.

Richman hurried to the hospital and was horrified when she got a first look at the dog. Flair was a bloody pulp. Nobody expected the dog to survive.

Veterinarian Amy Lockwood tended to Flair's gaping wounds, sewing 150 stitches in her neck and chest areas. Three tubes drained the poison from her flesh. Ron was inconsolable. He covered his face with his hands, ashamed that he had failed to protect Flair. He cried out that he had failed her and that he needed to give her to someone who could protect her. If she lived, he wanted her safe and with someone who wouldn't let any harm come to her.

After seeing to Flair's wounds, Ron was then taken to the emergency room, treated with tranquilizers, and released that same night. In the days that followed, word spread about the vicious attack. Friends and CCI supporters banded together to support Ron and Flair. Cards poured in by the dozens, and Ron taped them to his living-room wall. But the drapes stayed closed. Ron stopped taking walks.

Flair's severe wounds required constant monitoring and care, so she went home with Richman for a few weeks. Ron didn't want to see Flair; he had made up his mind to find her a new home, a safe home where no harm could find her. No one could convince him that the same thing could happen to any of them. No one and no words could make it all right.

Silently, Ron mourned her death, even as Flair's wounds healed. Her spirit healed, too. She was slowly introduced to other dogs, starting with a few days back home with her mother, Nadia.

Nadia remembered Flair. She remembered that this was her baby and that something was very wrong. Mom gently cajoled Flair, finally getting her to wag her tail and join in the fun.

A few days later, more dogs came to the ranch where Flair was raised. She became her old self, back to a "glass-is-always-half-full" kind of dog. It was time for her to go home.

But Ron wasn't convinced. He had mourned her and finally settled into a dark funk where no one, not even Flair, could reach him.

In the end, it was Ron who would have to reach out and save Flair. She became lethargic and sickly. Tests revealed nothing; her body was sound. Staff at the clinic who had once called Flair their miracle dog admitted that it looked as if she needed a second miracle.

Richman is convinced that, emotionally, Ron had pushed Flair out of his life and she had lost the will to live. She said she had never seen a dog so attuned to its owner's emotions. Flair needed Ron; he was her life.

People who knew Ron and Flair weren't surprised and told him so. In the past, Flair got upset whenever she felt that Ron was upset. Now, they told Ron, it was time for him to be there for Flair.

On a cloudy Monday morning, Ron opened his home and his heart to Flair. She bounded into the room and was back to her old self within days. They're a team again, a "glass-is-always-half-full" kind of team, invincible and inseparable to the end.

LOVE HEELS • Tales from Canine Companions for Independence

Hearing Teams

Because it charges its clients nothing for its dogs, all roads led to Canine Companions for Independence. The organization cross-trains dogs for both signal and balance.

Hearing Team This team pairs adults who are hard of hearing or deaf with Canine Companions to alert them to everyday sounds such as doorbells, alarm clocks, and smoke alarms. 🐾

A Family Affair

Two men reached out to grab her shoulder, hoping to pull the woman from the path of the speeding car. Natalie Woods-Sproule never heard the squealing tires, never heard the chorus of warnings from the strangers in the crosswalk just three paces behind her. But her Labrador retriever heard the whine of the metal monster and pushed Natalie out of harm's way.

The crowd watched in horror, their worst fears punctuated by a harsh thud. "I was on a business trip in Washington, D.C., my first big trip since I was paired with my hearing dog Barack," Natalie remembers. "I felt awkward eating in a restaurant alone, so I went out to get a sandwich at a deli near the train station. I was on my way back to the hotel when the car rounded a corner out of nowhere."

The crowd rushed to the side of the woman and her dog. Natalie was unhurt, but Barack's tail was bent and tender. The shiny black Lab kept her eyes on Natalie, ignoring the crowd hovering around them. A spot check of Barack proved that nothing was bleeding or broken. Back in the safety of their hotel room, Natalie munched on a ham-and-cheese with one hand and stroked Barack with the other.

"It is only with the heart that one can see rightly; what is essential is invisible to the eye." —Antoine de Saint-Exupéry

Barack, Natalie smiles, has changed a lot of things in her life in the five years since they became a team. It was because of the dog that Natalie met Dennis Sproule in the spring of 1997. Both had signed on for hearing dogs from Canine Companions for Independence and spent two weeks at the Santa Rosa, California, campus learning to work with their new partners. Their two dogs, Barack and

Harris, were old pals and liked being around each other as much as Dennis and Natalie enjoyed each other's company.

Their lives had been as different as their degree of hearing loss. Natalie lost her hearing as an adult; Dennis was born with a severe hearing impairment. Two bouts of Bell's palsy in as many years robbed Natalie of her perfect pitch. The final blow was dealt by a particularly bad strain of Hong Kong flu. She woke up one morning to a silent world. She was twenty-seven years young. "My passion was music," Natalie says. "I grew up harmonizing with my mom and sister, and I miss hearing beautiful music. The hardest thing, though, is not being able to hear my husband, my two daughters, or my grandchildren."

It was Natalie's oldest daughter, Naidene, who suggested a service dog. Both of her daughters were on their own, and Natalie was living alone for the first time. She didn't like going out by herself and tended to withdraw from people when she wasn't working as an administrative specialist with the federal government. Natalie said she loved her job working with high-tech equipment—except on those occasions when her job required that she travel. "When I was away from home, I just rested with one hand on the nightstand so I could feel the vibration of the telephone when it rang," she says. "I couldn't sleep. I was concerned that someone might come into my hotel room or that there might be a fire and I wouldn't hear the smoke alarms."

The idea of teaming with a hearing dog appealed to Natalie. She filled out the required application, passed her interview, and received the call to come in for training in less than six months. Dennis Sproule, director of special education for the Norwalk-La Mirada Unified School District in California, waited two years for the same call. His hearing is minimal, even with powerful hearing aids. And, like Natalie, his

job requires that he spend a lot of time on the road.

In the days before he got his dog, Dennis insisted on keeping his hearing aids on all night while on the road, and that meant sitting up in a chair. He reiterated Natalie's concern about not being able to hear alarms, especially the smoke alarm. His home was fitted with special equipment, flashing lights, and vibrating alarms. But on the road, he felt vulnerable. "My friend Perry convinced me that I needed some type of assistance because of all the traveling I was doing," Dennis says. A Canine Companion seemed like the perfect solution for a life of improved independence. Both Dennis and Natalie arrived at the Santa Rosa campus in May of 1997.

The training was like going back to school, Natalie says. There was a lot to learn and tests to take to confirm that they had the knowledge necessary to successfully team with a Canine Companion. Going back to school after so many years away from a structured environment was hard enough. But the real test, she says, was having to focus on herself during training. "I had spent my life focusing on other people. I had to focus on myself, my needs, my abilities as well as my disabilities."

Eight CCI dogs were ready for partners—four were the smaller corgi breed and four were large breeds, either Labradors or golden retrievers. "I found a corgi too small. My vision isn't great with a smaller dog at my side," Natalie says. "The retrievers were too spirited. Then there was Barack, just my speed. Slow."

Dennis, on the other hand, had his eyes focused on a corgi. He wanted a traveling companion who could fit comfortably under his airplane seat. But he was concerned about the corgi's short legs and wondered if the dog would be able to keep up with his long strides. "The trainers took me outside for a test run, and the corgi easily kept pace with me," Dennis says. "I was slowing down before the dog."

Dennis and Natalie had struck up a friendship during training and exchanged e-mail addresses, promising to keep tabs on each other's progress. The early e-mails were all about Harris and Barack. Three months later, the e-mails were all about Dennis and Natalie. Three years later, Natalie and Barack strolled down the aisle and into the arms of a waiting Dennis with Harris by his side.

Dennis, who moves through life in two gears (fast and faster), and Natalie, who likes it fine in the slow lane, are traveling the same road. The fit is perfect, they say, because neither person wants to change the other. Even their dogs have settled in and accepted their differences. When Natalie removes Barack's leash and harness, the Lab becomes as wild as a Tasmanian devil, earning her the nickname Taz. But once she's back at work at Natalie's side, Barack shifts back into low gear. Natalie laughs that it's funny to watch the Taz turn into a turtle.

Harris takes her work seriously and answers the call to duty; her alerts are as fast and sure as a lead ball shot from a cannon. Dennis taught Harris to alert him whenever the dog hears someone calling his name. In the past, Dennis missed important conversations when he couldn't see the person's face to lip-read. "On several occasions parents have felt I was ignoring them, but the truth is, I couldn't hear them," Dennis says. "When I got Harris and trained her to alert for name recognition, that problem went away."

Harris was trained to ignore the telephone rings in Dennis's office and alert him to the buzz of the intercom instead. With five secretaries and twice the phone lines, Harris would be alerting Dennis every other minute. "And you can't ignore Harris's alert. She makes sure of that."

In the morning, twenty-three pounds of get-up-and-go pounces on Dennis's chest the moment the alarm clock buzzes. Harris puts her two paws on Dennis and stands there until he asks, "What?" Then she jumps off the bed, heads for the alarm, and lies down. "And Harris doesn't come with a snooze button," Dennis laughs. Barack, by contrast, gives Natalie a gentle nudge in the morning when her alarm clock goes off; either that or a lick.

Like most corgis, Harris has a habit of rolling over on her back with her four legs straight up in the air, especially when she's bored. She assumed that position during a particularly long and arduous school board meeting, something that didn't escape the attention of the board president. He moved the meeting along and now uses Harris as a bore barometer. Harris's sister Hazelton also has a short attention span when people get long-winded. "Hazelton was placed with Fresno minister George Posthumus," Dennis says. "She sits in the front row with his wife and rolls over the moment he starts his sermon. She stays snoozing on her back until she hears him say 'Amen,' then she springs back to life."

Kitchen timers, tea-kettle whistles, and microwave bells are no problem for the Sproules. Their four-legged kids are ready to alert the person in charge. The dogs don't even have to be in the kitchen, Natalie says. They just seem to know which of them needs to be alerted. "When Dennis puts popcorn in the microwave, Harris answers the bell and gets Dennis," Natalie says. "It's the same for Barack when I'm making popcorn. I swear the two of them talk and decide who's going to take care of what. One of them will be with us at all times. One takes a rest while the other stands duty."

The Woods-Sproule household, according to Natalie, has four hearts "but only one soul."

Elaine and Tawny

Elaine Dechter had seen the caped puppies in parades, had watched TV stories about them, and had marveled at how anyone could raise a Canine Companion and then give it up. She knew she couldn't. And had she even considered the idea of raising one, there wasn't the time. Chasing a toddler around the house had left her tired, and no amount of puppy love could energize her like an afternoon nap.

Just age, she told herself on that summer afternoon a dozen years ago. She grabbed a nap on the couch while her two-year-old daughter, Ilana, slept in her crib.

Elaine woke up, her head spinning. Her legs gave way; vertigo kept her horizontal until late afternoon. She thought it was a bout of the flu and shrugged it off. A good night's sleep would make her achy body as good as new, she said to herself.

"Success has nothing to do with what you gain in life or accomplish for yourself. It's what you do for others." —Danny Thomas

At bedtime, Elaine read a short story to Ilana, tucked her in, and said "Sweet dreams" to her husband, Chris Dunkle.

And that was the last time she heard her husband's husky laugh or her daughter's timid giggle, or even her own voice. At age thirty-seven, she had lost her hearing to an autoimmune inner-ear disease. She also lost her sense of balance and had to struggle to walk again.

The long road back to something like normalcy was arduous. Elaine didn't know how to read lips, but she could read her daughter's nonverbal demands. She turned their lack of verbal communication into a game, learning sign language from a book and then teaching it to her daughter. Ilana's first words were "milk" and "cookies."

Elaine's, too.

Doing their best to lead the life they had led before Elaine's disease struck, the family went on outings and even once to a holiday parade where a group of puppy raisers marched their charges down the middle of the street. For the first time, Elaine noticed that some of the dogs wore capes that showed they were hearing dogs.

Life was good again. Maybe a little lonely, but it was good. Then Elaine's lack of balance got so bad that she felt like a prisoner in her own home. Her physician tried to persuade Elaine to use a walker for balance, but she balked at the idea. Using a walker was a slippery slope; she'd seen it too many times. Within months, people at the clinic traded walkers for wheelchairs. She wasn't going to have any part of it.

located less than six miles from her home. The organization cross-trains dogs for both signal and balance, something her disability required if she was to regain her independence. She liked the required follow-up programs, which were designed to offer extra training throughout the working life of the dog.

She signed up and began what would turn out to be a three-year wait. She watched the puppies training at shopping centers and grocery stores. But the puppies didn't touch her heart as deeply as the faces of the puppy raisers. She marveled at how deeply they loved their young charges; she admired their willingness to help a stranger with a disability by giving up their puppy. How would she ever be able to thank her puppy raiser? she wondered.

Elaine got the call in August of 1997. After two

As for Tawny, she's like one of her kids, Elaine laughs. Tawny is her permanent toddler who loves her all the time.

Elaine traveled to Boston to attend a convention for "late-deafened adults," people who've gone deaf after they've acquired a primary language. One of the demonstrations showcased the benefits of having a signal dog; it was there that she said she fell in love with a Canine Companion. She returned home with a short list of organizations that trained hearing dogs.

She investigated several groups. Some were far away and wanted people to pay up to $25,000 for a trained dog. Other groups offered to train a signal dog for pay; the catch was that the person had to provide the dog. Elaine said she had neither the $25,000 nor the confidence that she could raise a dog that could be taught to signal train.

Because it charges its clients nothing for its dogs, all roads led to Canine Companions for Independence, Elaine says. The Santa Rosa group was

rigorous weeks of team training, she felt ready and able to work with Tawny on her own. The petite yellow Labrador was a perfect match, and, in the years that followed, she would save Elaine from some potentially nasty falls. The two ventured out and explored their new world.

Before Tawny, Elaine had to wait for Chris to come home from work so he could walk her next door to visit with a neighbor. There were no strolls on the beach or short trips to the corner store. She didn't go anywhere without someone's help.

Since Tawny, the two have carved out an active life. An avid knitter, Elaine teaches others the art and looks forward to the annual convention, which attracts more than 7,000 people. The two make their way around the convention floor and have become celebrities of sorts. Elaine, you see, is the only one

enough money in the world to thank CCI for giving her back her independence.

Tawny also serves as a bridge between mother and teen. While some kids feel embarrassed when a parent is around, Ilana points to her mom with pride. Her mom is the one with the "cool" dog. In addition, Ilana fosters Canine Companion puppies whenever she's asked to help. Elaine marvels at how completely her daughter loves each dog; this from the girl who once was afraid to go near a dog. She is amazed at her daughter's courage and tenderness.

As for Tawny, she's like one of her kids, Elaine laughs. Tawny is her permanent toddler who loves her all the time. Elaine's friends credit the dog with giving them back their old friend. She withdrew in the months and years after she went deaf and didn't really open up again until Tawny came into her life.

Looking back, Elaine admits that she closed off her world because she tired of trying to communicate with people. She felt both frustrated and rebuffed because she had to ask people to repeat words so often. But with a dog around, people seem to have infinite patience, she says. They're waiting for a chance to pet the dog.

Elaine calls Tawny her California girl because she's all touchy feely, especially when she catches sight of her puppy raiser, Emily Williams. Then Tawny goes nuts. They never forget their puppy raisers, Elaine says. And she never will, either; not Emily nor the army of volunteers who raise these four-legged miracles one puppy at a time.

there with a yellow Lab. People love to stop Tawny to say hello; some even know Elaine by name, too.

Tawny saved Elaine from a severe injury last year by pinning her against the wall on a stairwell. Halfway down, Elaine's legs quivered and weakened, but Tawny knew what to do to help her until she regained her balance. Life is better than she ever thought it could be since that nap nearly a dozen years ago.

Recently the two participated in a walk to raise money for various charities; Elaine and Tawny collected pledges for CCI. But, she says, there's not

Volunteers

The reality of CCI centers around the love that develops between dogs and people. It is an antidote to the negativity in the world.

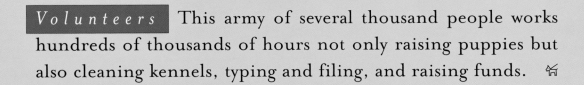

Volunteers This army of several thousand people works hundreds of thousands of hours not only raising puppies but also cleaning kennels, typing and filing, and raising funds. 🐕

Run for the Money

Kay Thompson hit the snooze button on her alarm clock, mentally recalculating the time it would take her to dress, drive, park, and perk up for the journey ahead. It was going to be a marathon day, literally.

The emergency-room nurse had a lot running on the race. She had spent months campaigning for contributions to pay for hammock-style cots to be placed in each of the kennels at the CCI Southwest Regional Center in Oceanside, California.

Life at the kennels is good; Thompson just wanted to make it cozier. To her way of thinking, nothing is too good for the canines camped at the center during their six months of advanced training. And nobody thought any different, so the pledges peaked at $146 per mile.

"When we accept tough jobs as a challenge to our ability and wade into them with joy and enthusiasm, miracles can happen." —Arland Gilbert

During those last few months before the 26.2-mile torturous trek, Thompson hit the road five days a week, sometimes covering ten miles, sometimes a little less. The months dwindled down to weeks, then days. The day of the race finally dawned.

Ready. Set. No go.

Just two more minutes, she bargained with the alarm clock. Her mind raced over the day's activities. Blood started coursing through her veins; she stretched and giggled. This marathon was different from the others she had run. She had nothing to prove, no time to beat, no milestone to reach. Thompson, like many other CCI volunteers, had figured out a simple truth: Whatever you give from the heart comes back and fills your own heart to overflowing.

That philosophy seemed plain enough, but like a lot of other simple truths, it was too complicated for some people to grasp. So a lot of people miss out, is the way Thompson figures it.

"How can you stand to give your puppy up?" "I would be too attached to my dog to ever let it go!" Thompson has heard these questions and expressions of disbelief over the four years and more that she has been a puppy raiser. Shima, a Labrador/golden retriever cross, is her fifth CCI pupil. This puppy is full of spunk, loves playing games, and is eager to

The drive up the coast was uneventful as the dashboard clock slowly ticked off the minutes. She parked her car and wiggled her way through the crowd until she found the start line.

Finally, the starting gun blasted. The race was on!

An early-morning fog slammed into her face, sending shivers down to the bone. It would be eight long and windy minutes before she spotted the first marker—one mile down and many more to go. Two, three, four, then five uneventful miles came and went.

In the distance, Thompson spotted the first of many yellow-caped canine markers that would send the soles of her feet soaring as high as her spirit. Four-legged cheerleaders barked on command until Thompson acknowledged that she had spotted them

She will tell you that she's truly grateful to be a part of the CCI mission to change lives one miracle at a time.

please. And someday, if she is very lucky, Shima will be paired with someone who needs that spunk to help him or her live a fuller life.

The seconds kept ticking on the clock, striking the present and condemning it to the past. A sleepy Thompson reached over the side of the bed to scratch behind Shima's ears. Shima responded with happy thumps of her tail. Shima and Holly, Kay Thompson's sister from Kansas City, would be cheering her on during the race and waiting for her at the end.

The alarm clock screamed at her, this time refusing to be silenced. Thompson bounded out of bed, grabbed her running shorts and sports top, and headed to the kitchen. She stretched her legs while her arms reached for a wheat bagel slathered with peanut butter. She was on the road in less than ten minutes—time to spare, she figured.

and headed their way.

The Canine Companion for Independence logo was embossed on Thompson's ruby red sports bra; paw prints along with the words "Running for Independence" were embroidered on the left side of her royal blue shorts. It was easy to spot Thompson from way down the block.

Puppy raisers and their canine charges were out by the dozens, shouting bravos and barks. Her cheerleaders had brought along a buffet of bagel bits, banana bars, and bottled water. Thompson paced herself, taking the time to pose for a snapshot with every service dog trainee along the route. The dogs knew, she later told friends, somehow they knew that she was doing this race for them. But then, friends counter, when the endorphins kick in, you don't have to make sense. Or maybe you have to be there, running the race and feeling the emotional surge, in

phone and called for help, begging for either single dollar bills or tissues at mile 13.

The sun warmed her body, making the sweat flow. And at every mile, the canines were there to lick off her salty sweat. Puppy love, Thompson swears, is high-octane fuel. She hugged the dogs, hugged their puppy raisers, and then raced off, heading for the next oasis of furry critters caped in blue and gold.

She found Camie at mile 13, a puppy she had helped foster while Camie's puppy raiser needed to take time away for a family emergency. Camie and her "Aunt Kay" were the best of pals; there was always joy beyond containment when their eyes met. And this time was no exception. The puppy pulled away from the crowd and raced to greet her. Thompson grabbed the leash and the two kept pace, Camie's tail moving faster than the runner's feet. This was a fun game, Camie's eyes shouted. Time for pictures, a hug, and then time ran out. Aunt Kay was gone without her, she whined.

Around the bend, she spotted Shima standing next to her sister. Shima bolted and headed for her. Again she set her pace to match the dog's until she reached Holly and another good friend, David, and a gift of pocket tissues.

Thompson's feet racked up the miles of money. There would be enough cash to purchase all the needed cots once she crossed the finish line. Her official race time was clocked at four hours and twelve minutes—26.2 miles of memories that added up to $3,825.20.

In the end, Thompson found herself surrounded by what she described as "the unique love that volunteering for CCI has brought to me." She will tell you that she's truly grateful to be a part of the CCI mission to change lives one miracle at a time. Today, though, the miracle belonged to her. It filled her heart to overflowing.

order to make sense of it all. No matter.

Even the euphoria couldn't block out reality, not by mile 12. All those sips, slurps, and slams of tea added up to one big problem. She borrowed a cell

If and Then

Diane Cruzen's eyes scanned a laundry list of "ifs," her heart sinking as she tallied the score. Any way she figured it, she couldn't meet the tough standards for board members.

It had been more than a year since Cruzen had heard about Canine Companions for Independence. She had meant to drop in at regional headquarters in Oceanside, California, to offer her time and talent. And money, too. But her job and other commitments kept her too busy.

"People never improve unless they look to some standard or example higher and better than themselves." —Tyron Edwards

But she made it, and even sat in on a board meeting with Southwest Regional Director Judith Pierson. Cruzen liked Pierson, liked the way the center was run and the money was spent. Volunteers played a big part in making the organization run; there were something like thirty volunteers for every paid staff member. She thought it was a good fit for her.

When her eyes glanced at the paper Pierson had folded in half and handed to her, she assumed it was a list of qualifications for the board. She was glad to get a heads up on what was expected.

"If you can start the day without caffeine or pep pills," the first line read.

Oh God, she remembers thinking. In trouble already. She liked to start her morning with a double latte. She shrugged her shoulders and vowed to kick the coffee habit. Water was better for her body anyway.

Then came, "If you can be cheerful, ignoring aches and pains."

"Okay, great, I can do that," she said to herself. She has learned to live with migraine headaches, and neither colds nor flu bugs sideline her. "I'm right in there," she said. "Yes sir, this rule was easy."

Next challenge, please.

"If you can resist complaining and boring people with your troubles."

"I can certainly do that," she grinned to herself. She didn't like complaining or hearing others complain. There are other ways, healthy ways, to expel frustrations. She kept on reading.

"If you can eat the same food every day and be grateful for it."

"Whoa, Houston, we have a problem," she silently balked. The smile faded from her lips. Food was her passion—no cuisine in particular, every cuisine in general. She began to feel uneasy and wondered what food had to do with being on the board. She made a mental note to eat whatever she liked and just not tell them.

Then came, "If you can understand when loved ones are too busy to give you time."

A self-described "sensitive" person, Cruzen wondered about this rule, too. People *do* have other interests and responsibilities, she said to herself. She knew she'd shed a few tears over this one but felt she could survive if she didn't take being ignored personally. She was shaky about where all this was going, but felt committed to keep reading.

"If you can overlook it when people take things out on you when, through no fault of yours, something goes wrong."

Nope. Never. Nada. Why should she take the blame when something wasn't her fault? Heck, she didn't even like taking the blame when something *was* her fault. Cruzen's ego had hit a barrier the size of Mount Everest, and there was no going over, around, through, or under it to make this work. She looked around and wondered just what kind of board this was. And what would she be signing up for if they *did* agree to let her join? She'd been on boards before, lots of boards. You showed up once a month and did a lot of work between meetings.

"The list was all about me and all my personal bad habits," she said later. "I wasn't happy, but I felt I had to read the whole thing and make an evaluation. I remember thinking I needed more freedom than this board allowed its members." She said she felt they were putting *her* on a leash, not the dogs.

In a last-ditch effort to make sense of it all, she reasoned that perhaps the board wanted new members to understand what it's like to be a companion animal. "I'm laughing now, but I'm serious," she says. "For a whole year CCI had been on my mind. I was so thrilled and excited to be a part of this organization. The thought of my being rejected before they met me, this was not acceptable to me."

She kept reading:

"If you can take criticism and blame without resentment,
If you can face the world without lies and deceit,
If you can conquer tension without medical help,
If you can relax without liquor,
If you can sleep without the aid of drugs,"

And that was the last sentence visible; the rest was on the other side of the folded paper. Pierson saw her reading the note and pushed it closer. Cruzen picked it up and turned it over, unable to hide her surprise when she read the last line:

"Then, you may be good enough to be a dog."

"Oh my God, oh my God, I don't believe it," she confessed. The joke was on her.

Thinking about it later, she wondered why she hadn't caught on after the fourth line, the one about eating the same food every day and being grateful for it. "Not even the pope eats the same food every day.

Nobody does," she says. "And who wouldn't mind being blamed for things that aren't his fault?"

It was then that she felt she'd found her place.

Cruzen agreed to chair the center's 2002 fall gala, the largest fundraiser for the southwest group.

"I love to laugh at myself and they got me!"

If you can start the day without caffeine or pep pills,

If you can be cheerful, ignoring aches and pains,

If you can resist complaining and boring people with your troubles,

If you can eat the same food every day and be grateful for it,

If you can understand when loved ones are too busy to give you time,

If you can overlook it when people take things out on you when, through no fault of yours, something goes wrong,

If you can take criticism and blame without resentment,

If you can face the world without lies and deceit,

If you can conquer tension without medical help,

If you can relax without liquor,

If you can sleep without the aid of drugs,

...then, you may be good enough to be a dog!

Helpful and Happy

The idea tugged at her heartstrings as strongly as fear gnawed at her belly. She had the time, she figured, and had the desire, too. But it was going to be scary.

A friend had come over for coffee and had brought along a pet project on a leash. Ruth Darby was training a puppy for a new organization called Canine Companions for Independence. Darby tied the dog to a post outside Bev Coke's home and came inside to recruit the recently retired schoolteacher. Coke confessed that she was terrified of dogs; had been since she was a small girl and a neighbor's pet took a bite out of her cheek. Her hand still rubs the small scar when she talks about that day and the days that followed.

"No one can sincerely try to help another without helping himself." —Charles Dudley Warner

Darby talked to her friend about the group and explained that it desperately needed volunteers to succeed in partnering people in wheelchairs with Canine Companions. "I just showed up the next day and have been showing up almost every day since," says Coke. "But don't ask me how I got so involved. I just don't know but I did."

That first day in the fall of 1983 was uneventful. It was late afternoon when she finally got up the nerve to drive over to the small frame house on Sebastopol Road used by CCI volunteers. She stood on the porch for an hour and watched them busily carrying out their duties. At 5 o'clock, everybody went home.

Coke returned the next morning. This time she spoke up and asked what she could do to help. She would be happy to do anything, she said, as long as she didn't

"These dogs were just different. I had watched them work with the trainers and I just fell in love with them all."

have to be near a dog.

Turned out there was plenty else to do, especially for someone as well organized and eager to help as she was. She was handed a thick computer printout book that listed names and addresses of movie stars. If the group was going to succeed, it needed some angels to fund the program.

Coke had spent her working years teaching fitness and sportsmanship to teens; computers were about as familiar to her as the smell of fresh air in a gym locker room. But she was game; Coke liked learning new things and attacked the project typing on a donated computer with shifty keys.

The days and weeks passed. Coke contacted stars for support and expanded her duties to all things paper, careful to keep away from the training end. She watched the dogs and admired the people who worked with them, but always from afar. She helped get the word out about the group, recruiting more volunteers and candidates for CCI. As time went on, she began to soften around the dogs, and even petted a few of them and offered treats. "These dogs were different," she says, "so sweet, so well mannered and loving."

The months passed, and soon the time came to pair the pups with people. Word of the program traveled fast, and people from all over the country signed up. A lucky few were selected and traveled to Santa Rosa to train for two arduous weeks.

The living room of the volunteers' house was converted into a training room. Come lunchtime, the room became the dining room. Coke and the others brought food from their home kitchens and set up card tables. There was always a hot casserole, fresh biscuits, and cookies. "We all just believed so deeply in the idea of these dogs helping people with disabilities become more independent that we were determined to do whatever it took to make it work," Coke says.

Soon, CCI had outgrown the small house, and the group settled into a dilapidated chicken coop, an old building full of loose boards and peeling paint. More volunteers were recruited to patch the building and make it usable. One end of the coop was set aside to whelp puppies; another was partitioned off for grooming. It was dark and dingy, and whenever the city inspector came to check it out, he always left shaking his head, Coke says. Plans were in the works to fix up the place, but with volunteers doing all the work it would take months.

A few times, the dogs wiggled their way out of the makeshift kennels and scattered in a nearby field. Coke ran with the others to round up the dogs and bring them home. She says she forgot about being afraid of the dogs; she was more concerned with their safety. She grabbed a few by the scruff of their necks and walked them back to the kennels. "These dogs were just different. I had watched them work with the trainers and I just fell in love with them all," she says. Another time, a litter of puppies got loose and scattered. She found herself hunting for the tiny bundles and carting them back in pairs.

When it rained, puddles dotted the straw floor. The only dry place in the building was where the puppies were tucked away. Everybody else worked in raincoats. "Everything in the place either was bought at yard sales or borrowed from volunteers," Coke says. "Once, during team training, the toilet began flooding the place and a student's husband fixed it while his wife worked with her dog." Lunchtime was always an adventure. Volunteers drove into the back of the building and used their car hoods as kitchen counter space.

Many graduates have come and gone through the CCI training program in the years since Coke signed on. She has her favorites; for example, the little girl from Canada who traveled to Santa Rosa with her mom and two teachers. "I believe the little girl was autistic," Coke says. "During class time, she would walk along the edge of the room and play a game by herself." She never could sleep all night; she would wander about. Her mom was relieved the first night the dog came home with them. In the middle of the night, she went to check on her daughter and found her fast asleep with her arm around the dog. "She said she knew life was going to change now that she had the dog to help look after her daughter," Coke smiles, adding that she personally knows of many stories with the same happy ending.

In April Coke celebrated her seventy-fifth birthday at a party on the Schulz campus in Santa Rosa. She works there five afternoons a week, a completely computer-literate mail carrier who handles all communications from the public and gets them where they need to go. All that, and she still manages to volunteer extra time making lunches during the team-training sessions held for two weeks during February, May, August, and November.

Coke retired once from teaching but says she'll never tire of helping team people and Canine Companions; she's in for the long haul. "I admire the people who raise and train the dogs. I still have never been able to bring myself to help with that side of the organization," she says. "But I do what I can and I love being here around so many wonderful people."

She did need to sit down and take a break after the last team-training luncheon, adding that she may have had to "sit down, but I'm not sitting it out."

The Life of a CCI Dog

1 Breeding

Mom's a star, dad's a stud, and the six of us are pretty good looking, if I do say so myself. And as if that weren't enough, we've got the ultimate weapon to conquer hearts—"puppy breath." All together now, "Aaahhhhhhhh." It's been a fun two months with Mom and the sibs, but I'm getting antsy and want a human all to myself. It's time to head out into the world. Woof!

2 Puppy raising

I'm lucky I'm so cute—two toileting accidents in two days. Hey, what do you want, I'm just a baby! This puppy job is pretty soft; I just put my butt on the ground when she says "Sit," and my human smiles all day. I heard her tell someone that I'm going to learn twenty-five commands in the next year or so. What's a command, and do I have to do it?

3 Advanced training

I can sit, stay, heel, jump, and shake paws, so now I'm off to college to learn some really hard skills like opening doors—even the refrigerator door. Oh boy, that's where humans keep the good kibble, like hamburgers and cheese. This is a piece of cake—um, I like cake, too.

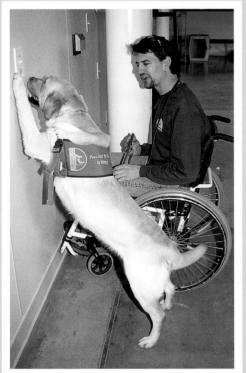

Release

Oops, the teacher called my parents today and told them to come and get me. See, I passed my eye, heart, and hip tests, but then they tripped me up with this tennis-ball test. I've never met a tennis ball that didn't have my name on it, so I just did what came naturally and chased it. Caught it, too. Foul ball, I'm told. Bad dog! See, these people have this rule about restraint and I just couldn't. Then they put peanut-butter cookies all over the training-room floor and expected me to walk around them. Yep, I flunked the taste test. I've said my goodbyes to my roomie, Gobi, so come and get me. My bags are packed. Love, Trish.

4 Team training

The six months are over and it's time to meet the new folks. I can't wait! I saw this really nice man, and he smiled at me when he said my name, Gobi. And this kid, she wheeled her chair near my kennel and spoke *so* softly. Somebody here needs me, and I need somebody here, too. By the end of this week I'll know which human will belong to me. We'll spend another week here working as a team and then head home. Goodie.

5 Service

It's easy to read my human. Sometimes Tom just has to look at me and I know what he needs. It's been this way from the beginning. Everywhere he goes, I go, because I'm part of the team. Workdays are long sometimes, but then there are the ball games and naps in front of the fire, so it all evens out. Last night Tom rolled over and then couldn't breathe, so I had to run and get help. Tom is my whole world, and he tells me the same thing. Life is good.

6 Retirement

Some days my legs just don't work well. My bones are getting creaky and my belly is getting soft. My heart says yes but my body says no. I'm twelve this week—that's eighty-four in human years. Tom and I have been together my whole adult life. How will he ever do without me? But I'm tired and Tom knows it. It's time to let a younger pup take over the work. As for me, I'll spend the rest of my days being adored and loved just for being me. Cool.

May God bless everyone associated with CCI; as for the dogs—they don't need blessing, for they are pure of heart and guaranteed the reward of Heaven's fields from the day that each is born. —Dean Koontz

CANINE COMPANIONS
FOR INDEPENDENCE

For further information, log on to CCI's Web site at www.cci.org or contact a regional center. Locations and telephone numbers are given at right.

Canine Companions for Independence National Headquarters and Northwest Regional Center Jean and Charles Schulz Campus

ADDRESS: 2965 Dutton Avenue
PO Box 446
Santa Rosa, CA 95402-0446
VOICE: (707) 577-1700
TTY: (707) 577-1756
TOLL FREE: (800) 572-BARK (2275)

Canine Companions for Independence's national head-quarters and Northwest Regional Center are located on the nearly thirteen-acre Schulz Campus in Santa Rosa, California. Since 1975, 744 teams have graduated from this center, which serves Washington, Oregon, Wyoming, Montana, Alaska, Idaho, northern California, and northern Nevada.

Each regional center has responsibility for all those in its area who are involved in Canine Companion activities: the graduates themselves, puppy raisers, applicants and candidates, breeder caretakers, volunteers, donors, and supporters. Throughout the northwest region, there are currently 234 puppy raisers and more than 1,000 dedicated CCI volunteers.

Southwest Regional Center
Dean and Gerda Koontz Campus

ADDRESS: 124 Rancho del Oro Drive
           PO Box 4568
           Oceanside, CA 92057-7344
VOICE: (760) 901-4300
TTY: (760) 901-4326
FAX: (760) 901-4350
TOLL FREE: (800) 572-BARK (2275)

The Southwest Regional Center has been making a difference in the lives of people with disabilities since 1986. It serves Arizona, Utah, Colorado, New Mexico, Texas, Oklahoma, Arkansas, Hawaii, southern California, and southern Nevada. Its satellite office is located in Colorado Springs, Colorado.

The Southwest Regional Center has placed 575 assistance dogs and currently has 187 puppy raisers and 550 active volunteers.

North Central Regional Center

ADDRESS: 4989 State Route 37 East
           Delaware, OH 43015-9682
VOICE/TTY: (740) 548-4447
FAX: (760) 363-0555
TOLL FREE: (800) 572-BARK (2275)

The North Central Regional Center of Canine Companions for Independence opened in 1987. Since that time, 362 teams have graduated. There are currently 115 puppy raisers and nearly 500 active volunteers supporting the services of CCI in this region. Its satellite office is located in Chicago. The North Central Region serves North Dakota, South Dakota, Nebraska, Kansas, Minnesota, Iowa, Missouri, Wisconsin, Illinois, Indiana, Michigan, Ohio, Kentucky, and western Pennsylvania.

Northeast Regional Center

ADDRESS: SUNY Farmingdale
           Farm Complex - Melville Road
           PO Box 205
           Farmingdale, NY 11735-0205
VOICE/TTY: (631) 694-6938
FAX: (631) 694-0308
TOLL FREE: (800) 572-BARK (2275)

After a few renovations, CCI will relocate its campus from its present location in Farmingdale to an eleven-acre site in Medford, on Long Island. The new facility includes an existing 30,000-square-foot building that will provide expanded kennels and office space as well as guest accommodations for participants and graduate teams.

The Farmingdale location was opened in 1989 and has graduated 308 teams. It has 97 puppy raisers in addition to another 200 active volunteers. This center serves Maine, New Hampshire, Vermont, New York, Massachusetts, Rhode Island, Connecticut, New Jersey, Delaware, Maryland, Washington, D.C., Virginia, West Virginia, and eastern Pennsylvania.

Southeast Regional Center
Anheuser-Busch/SeaWorld Campus

ADDRESS: 8150 Clarcona Ocoee Road
           PO Box 680388
           Orlando, FL 32868-0388
VOICE: (407) 522-3300
FAX: (407) 522-3347
TOLL FREE: (800) 572-BARK (2275)

The Southeast Regional Center was founded in 1989 in Orlando and held its first team training in the fall of 1995. The new campus opened its doors on July 4, 2000, and has graduated 193 teams. There are currently 70 active puppy raisers and 500 regional volunteers in eight states: Alabama, Florida, Georgia, Louisiana, Mississippi, North Carolina, South Carolina, and Tennessee.

 Acknowledgments

We are grateful to the many people who participated in this project – from all those who agreed to be interviewed and share their CCI stories, to the artists and photographers who helped bring the book to life.

The foreword to the book, written by **Dean Koontz** is a beautiful tribute to CCI, and we thank him for being such an important part of this project.

A very special thanks to artist **Ron Burns** for his generosity in creating the beautiful and soulful painting of the CCI dog for the cover and the paw and heart artwork that runs throughout the book. To view more of Ron's artwork please visit his Web site: **www.ronburns.com**

A thank-you to **Jean Schulz** and **Charles M. Schulz Creative Associates** for granting us permission to use the Peanuts cartoon that appears on the endsheets of the book. We are so very honored to have the work of the great Charles Schulz, CCI supporter, included in this book.

Special thanks to **Greg Evans** for allowing his Luann cartoon to be reprinted in the book and sharing the story of the creation of his CCI series.

Thanks also to the artists whose drawings accompany stories in the book: the drawing of Blanche on page 79 is copyrighted © by **Lynn Stallard**, and the drawing of Romer on page 123 is copyrighted © by **Dena Mangiamele**.

Picture Credits

The photographs that appear on pages 3, 6, 10, 13, 14, 15, 18, 23-26, 32, 33, 36, 38-41, 53, 72, 73, 94, 95, 112-114, 124-127, 178, 179, 193, 204, 210, 211 212, 214, 216-221, and are the property of Canine Companions for Independence.

The photograph that appears on page 24, is by Tofer Cox and reprinted in this book with the permission of CCI.

The photographs that appear on pages 16, 19, 20, 28, 34, 35, 37, 74, 80, 81, 83, 97, 115-117, 119, 136, 137, 139, 146, 148, 149, 150, 159, 160, 163, 205-207, 209, 216, 217, 219, 220, are copyrighted © by Kevin Nelson and were created especially for this book.

The photographs that appear on pages 14, 15, 21, 22, 50, 51, 72, 96, 156-158, 168-170, 190-192, 202, 203 are copyrighted © by Marshall Harrington and reprinted in this book with the permission of the photographer.

The photographs that appear on pages 54, 57, 65, 73, 76, 128, 129, 131, 187, 188, and 216 are copyrighted © by Barbara S. Martin and reprinted in this book with the permission of the photographer.

Grateful acknowledgment is made to the following people and their families for use of their photographs that appear in the book: Sue Calvano: pages 64, 66, 67; Joanne Cohn: pages 42, 47, 216; the Cole family: pages 140, 142; Willie Crawford: pages 74, 75, 77; Karen and Tim Daynes: pages 27, 176, 181; Elaine Dechter: pages 198, 201; Patricia Dibsie: pages 60, 62, 108, 111; Carolyn Edwards: pages 182, 185; the Flynn family: pages 17, 29-31, 52, 73, 84-89, 216; Jim Gahen: pages 104, 105, 107; Tom Hollenstein: page 172; Owen and Harry Kent: page 144; Diana Klein: pages 133, 135; Judy Myers: page 152; Cathy Phillips: pages 44-46, 48; Darla Reed: pages 98-101, 103; Barbara Richman: page 120; Bill Roth: pages 173, 175; Sally Simcoe: pages 164, 165, 167; Natalie and Dennis Sproule: page 194; Annie Williams: pages 68, 71.

The photograph of Dean Koontz and Trixie on page 8 is copyrighted © by J. Bauer and used with permission.

The photograph that appears on page 58 is copyrighted © and is reprinted with permission from the Deseret News.

Art Credit: The Peanuts cartoon that appears on the endsheets of this book is copyrighted © by United Features Syndicate, Inc., 1996.

Text Credit: The story "The Long Goodbye" was reprinted with permission from The San Diego Union Tribune.